Curriculum Design, Evaluation, and Teaching in Medical Education

Jochanan Benbassat

Curriculum Design, Evaluation, and Teaching in Medical Education

Recognizing Challenges and Opportunities

Jochanan Benbassat
Department of Medicine (retired)
Hadassah-Hebrew University Medical School
Jerusalem, Israel

ISBN 978-3-031-76844-6   ISBN 978-3-031-76845-3 (eBook)
https://doi.org/10.1007/978-3-031-76845-3

© The Editor(s) (if applicable) and The Author(s), under exclusive license to Springer Nature Switzerland AG 2024

This work is subject to copyright. All rights are solely and exclusively licensed by the Publisher, whether the whole or part of the material is concerned, specifically the rights of translation, reprinting, reuse of illustrations, recitation, broadcasting, reproduction on microfilms or in any other physical way, and transmission or information storage and retrieval, electronic adaptation, computer software, or by similar or dissimilar methodology now known or hereafter developed.

The use of general descriptive names, registered names, trademarks, service marks, etc. in this publication does not imply, even in the absence of a specific statement, that such names are exempt from the relevant protective laws and regulations and therefore free for general use.

The publisher, the authors and the editors are safe to assume that the advice and information in this book are believed to be true and accurate at the date of publication. Neither the publisher nor the authors or the editors give a warranty, expressed or implied, with respect to the material contained herein or for any errors or omissions that may have been made. The publisher remains neutral with regard to jurisdictional claims in published maps and institutional affiliations.

Editorial Contact: Richard Lansing

This Springer imprint is published by the registered company Springer Nature Switzerland AG

The registered company address is: Gewerbestrasse 11, 6330 Cham, Switzerland

If disposing of this product, please recycle the paper.

*To Niall Byrne, Arthur I. Rothman, and
Richard Tiberius—mentors and friends*

Preface

In 1979, the Dean of the Hadassah-Hebrew University School of Medicine asked me to take over as head of the Medical Education Unit (MEU). I had already been on the staff of the Department of Medicine for ten years, and the Dean felt that my clinical capability and interest in medical education made me suitable for the position. To consider his offer, I spent a year at the Division of Medical Education at the University of Toronto and took a course entitled "Curriculum in Institutions of Higher Education." The goal of the course was to get students to integrate educational theory and practice, to look at education as a field of research, and to examine curriculum design in medical schools in general and problem-based learning in particular.

After taking this course and visiting several MEUs in North America, I realized that just as in other university departments, the function of MEUs depends on their members' views, knowledge, and creativity. But unlike other university departments, it also depends on the relationship with customers—deans and faculty. Being sensibly modest about my ability to build such relationships and aware of my other limitations, I declined the dean's offer and continued my clinical work until I retired. Nevertheless, I maintained my interest in education, particularly in teaching basic clinical skills to medical students and introducing them to clinical reasoning and the psychosocial determinants of disease.

This book summarizes my experience in Ontario which influenced my approach to teaching and the views I have held since. Of course, it is not intended to inform education experts and does not attempt to suggest to MEU members how to meet the needs and expectations of teachers. However, I hope this guide will interest academic physicians who share my interest in clinical teaching. I would like to thank Drs. R. Baumal, R. Cohen, J. Lubsen, and J.A. Van, co-authors of earlier versions of the various sections, and the journals that published them, for granting me permission to include their updated versions in this book.

Jerusalem, Israel   Jochanan Benbassat

Contents

1 Purpose and Function of Institutions of Higher Education 1
   1.1 Definitions 2
      1.1.1 Education 2
      1.1.2 Education vs Training 2
      1.1.3 Education, Conditioning, and Indoctrination........... 3
      1.1.4 Learning for Various Degrees of Proficiency........... 3
   1.2 Purpose of Higher Education................................ 3
      1.2.1 Goals of Higher Education........................... 4
   1.3 Institutions of Higher Education 8
   1.4 Summing up.. 9
   References... 9

2 Curriculum Design 13
   2.1 The Curriculum as a Teaching Program 13
      2.1.1 Components of a Teaching Program: Knowledge,
           Skills, and Attitudes................................ 13
      2.1.2 Structure of a Teaching Program: Prerequisites.......... 14
      2.1.3 Structure of a Teaching Program: Learning Objectives.... 15
   2.2 The Curriculum as a Process 16
      2.2.1 Student-Centered Vs Teacher-Centered Models 17
      2.2.2 Matching and Developmental Models.................. 19
   2.3 The Curriculum as an All-Inclusive Statement 19
      2.3.1 Context.. 19
      2.3.2 Input.. 20
      2.3.3 Process.. 20
      2.3.4 Product.. 22
   References... 22

3 The Evaluation of the Medical Curriculum 25
   3.1 The Need for Curriculum Evaluation......................... 25
   3.2 Models of Evaluation of Medical Curricula 26

		3.2.1	Evaluation of the Need for the Curriculum	26
		3.2.2	End-Product Evaluation	27
		3.2.3	Process Evaluation	28
	3.3	Attitudes and Values in Curriculum Evaluations		31
		3.3.1	Values of Evaluators	31
		3.3.2	Faculty Values	32
		3.3.3	Values of Medical Students	32
	3.4	Summing Up		33
		3.4.1	Improvement of Instruments for Curriculum Evaluation	33
		3.4.2	Comprehensive Summative Examination and Counseling of Medical Students	34
	References			34
4	**Quality Control of Education**			**37**
	4.1	Medical Education Units		37
	4.2	External Reviews for Accreditation of Medical Schools		38
	4.3	Prioritization of Accreditation Standards		39
		4.3.1	Level 1: The Most Important Accreditation Standards	40
		4.3.2	Level 2: Important Standards	42
		4.3.3	Level 3: Possibly Important Standards	42
		4.3.4	Level 4: Least Important Standards	43
	4.4	Summing Up		43
	References			44
5	**Curriculum Innovations and Alternative Models of Medical Education**			**47**
	5.1	Theoretical Models of Disease and Medical Training		47
	5.2	The Problem-Based, Self-Directed Learning Model		48
	5.3	Early Student Exposure to Patients		49
	5.4	Longitudinal Integrated Clerkships		49
	5.5	Teaching Clinical Reasoning (See Also Sect. 9.6)		51
	5.6	Summing Up		52
	References			52
6	**Patient Care, Teaching, and Research**			**55**
	6.1	Assessment of Research and Teaching in Higher Education		55
		6.1.1	Assessment of Research Productivity	55
		6.1.2	Assessment of Teaching Performance	56
	6.2	Teaching and/or vs Research		57
	6.3	The Case for Including Science Education in the Undergraduate Curriculum		58
		6.3.1	Objectives of Science Education	58
		6.3.2	Similarity Between Scientific Research and Clinical Problem-Solving	59
		6.3.3	Summing Up	59

	6.4	Clinician-Scientists	60
		6.4.1 Reasons for the Declining Numbers of Clinician-Scientists	61
		6.4.2 Clinician-Scientists: Difficulties Maintaining the Dual Role	62
		6.4.3 Projections for the Future........................	62
	References..		63
7	**Social Influences on Education, Research, and Healthcare**		65
	7.1	Objectivism and Relativism..............................	65
	7.2	Levels of Scientific Evidence.............................	66
	7.3	Social Influences on Knowledge and Beliefs.................	66
		7.3.1 Social Influences on Research	66
		7.3.2 Social Influences on Health Care...................	67
	7.4	Complementary/Alternative Medicine......................	68
		7.4.1 Utilization of Complementary and Alternative Medicine	69
		7.4.2 The p-Value Fallacy.............................	70
		7.4.3 Conclusions	71
	References..		73
8	**Often Neglected Guidelines for Clinical Practice, Teaching, and Further Inquiry**		75
	8.1	Neglected Guidelines for Clinical Practice	76
		8.1.1 Identify the Patient's Concerns and Expectations	76
		8.1.2 Encourage Patients to Seek a Second Opinion	77
		8.1.3 Underprivileged Patients Are at Higher Risk for Morbidity	77
		8.1.4 Be Aware of the Causes of Patient Dissatisfaction with Doctors...................................	78
	8.2	Neglected Guidelines for Teaching	79
		8.2.1 Teach Basic Clinical Skills and Patient Counseling for Mastery....................................	79
		8.2.2 Caution Students from Unselective Imitation of Role Models.................................	81
		8.2.3 Make Students Aware of Medical Errors...............	81
		8.2.4 Medical Error Teaching Programs...................	82
		8.2.5 Doctors' Response to the Awareness they Committed an Error	84
		8.2.6 Professional Distress	85
		8.2.7 Inconsistencies Between Theory and Practice...........	85
	References..		86
9	**Issues that May Require Curricular Changes**		91
	9.1	Selection of Applicants for Undergraduate Medical Training	92
		9.1.1 The Problem....................................	92
		9.1.2 Non-cognitive Attributes: Advantages and Limitations....	93

		9.1.3 Competing Values	96
		9.1.4 Conclusions	96
	9.2	Personalizing Medical Education and Reducing its Duration	98
	9.3	Furthering Student Well-being	100
	9.4	Managing Time-Constrained Doctor-Patient Encounters	100
	9.5	Teaching the Social and Behavioral Sciences	102
	9.6	Teaching Clinical Reasoning and Coping with Uncertainty	103
		9.6.1 The Hypothesis-Driven Physical Examination	104
		9.6.2 Doctors' Problem-Solving Strategies	104
		9.6.3 Barriers to Learning Clinical Reasoning	105
		9.6.4 Assessment of Clinical Reasoning	106
		9.6.5 Summing Up	106
	9.7	Dealing with Unprofessional Behavior	107
	9.8	Teamwork	108
	9.9	Private Care in Countries with Universal Health Insurance	110
		9.9.1 Ethical Issues	110
		9.9.2 Other Issues	111
		9.9.3 Private Care in Public Institutions: Effect on Role Modeling	111
		9.9.4 "Black" Medicine	112
		9.9.5 Suggestions for Improvement	112
	9.10	Evaluation and Counseling of Medical School Graduates	112
	References		113
Index			121

Chapter 1
Purpose and Function of Institutions of Higher Education

Abstract The term "higher education" refers to learning in post-secondary institutions such as universities and colleges. Its purpose is to explore the world of knowledge, foster reflective capacity, train the workforce, prepare for a career, and promote personal and regional development. Universities try to achieve this by combining applied research and educating a new generation of citizens and leaders.

Another purpose of higher education is to promote personal development such as epistemological growth, tolerance of uncertainty, moral reasoning, empathy, emotional intelligence, and the capacity for reflection. However, studies of the changes in these traits during higher education have yielded mixed results. On the one hand, graduate students have been reported to have higher levels of *epistemological development* than undergraduate students. *Moral reasoning* scores increase during college, nursing, physical therapy, and pharmacy education but not in computer science and medical students. Similarly, most cross-sectional and longitudinal studies of medical students and residents found a decline in *empathy* test scores.

A statement describing higher education institutions should include their context and function. The context refers to the academic freedom of the faculty, funding, and the stakeholders to whom it is accountable. The function of a higher education institution refers to its mission and goals. The wording of a mission statement is intentionally vague to ensure consistency between different departments. Therefore, it does not define specific teaching programs. Implementing such programs requires their translation into learning objectives that define the expectations from of the graduate. The more detailed these are, the more targeted the teaching and the assessment of its outcomes can be. By analogy, travelers in an unfamiliar country need a large-scale map to know where they are going (institutional goals) and a detailed topographical map to understand how to get there (learning objectives).

1.1 Definitions

1.1.1 Education

Like other terms in a natural language, the term "education" developed a "life of its own and sprouted offshoots that took it far away from the central trunk of the concept" (Peters 1966). Education has a double meaning. The first is a *process* involving teachers and learners; the second is an *achievement* that implies a change in the learner's state of mind. Conventional wisdom defines "education" as teaching someone something. But teaching someone how to cheat is not education; teaching math is. Therefore, Peters expanded the definition to "teaching someone something worthwhile." What is considered worthwhile depends on social norms (see Chapter. 7): Math and chess are worthwhile, poker is not, and playing bridge is controversial. But even the latter definition seems incomplete: Teaching children arithmetic by punishing them when they make mistakes is not education. Therefore, the definition should be "To teach someone something worthwhile by methods acceptable by today's ethical standards" (Peters 1966). Education is a value-laden statement about what and how it is taught. This subsection further defines the term education and the levels of achievement expected of learners.

1.1.2 Education vs Training

Although the terms education and training are often used interchangeably, they refer to activities with different goals. "Training" aims to impart certain skills and suggests a competence of limited scope, while education also encompasses knowledge and values and implies that a person's whole attitude has changed. Training consists of imitation, while education encourages critical reflection (Calman and Downie 1988). These different definitions lead to different interpretations of the value of role modeling. If defined as training, then role modeling is essential. However, if described as the unreflective imitation of role models by learners and the uncritical adoption of the messages of the learning environment, then the benefits of role modeling may be outweighed by its unintended harms. The imitation of role models can encourage undesirable practices, such as doctor-centered patient interviewing. Therefore, it is important to caution students against uncritically imitating role models and to encourage them to judiciously evaluate their teachers' behavior and the learning environment's messages (Benbassat 2014).

1.1.3 Education, Conditioning, and Indoctrination

Indoctrination means taking advantage of a privileged role to influence one's subordinates through conditioning and brainwashing. Conditioning is considered acceptable for training when rational methods are not possible, e.g., with very young children. Brainwashing uses all known methods, such as conditioning, fear, anxiety, distortions, and drugs, to change a person's patterns of thinking and feeling. Both indoctrination and education attempt to change a person's attitude (Calman and Downie 1988). However, they differ in purpose and method. Education encourages critical reflection; indoctrination distorts learners' ability to evaluate evidence. Education uses morally acceptable methods; indoctrination uses brainwashing, fear, or coercion.

1.1.4 Learning for Various Degrees of Proficiency

Until the 1960s, the goal of undergraduate medical education was to produce graduates capable of unsupervised primary care. Today, medical school graduates need additional residency training to acquire the ability to practice unsupervised. However, members of curriculum committees seem to have difficulty in discerning between their expectations of medical students and residents. Differing viewpoints lead to disagreements about the objectives of undergraduate clinical education and the level required of medical school graduates: what should be taught for general knowledge only, for mastery, or for intermediate levels of proficiency.

The concept of learning for mastery was introduced by Bloom in 1968. Its unique features stem from the view that uncorrected errors lead to learning difficulties. Therefore, it begins by dividing the learning material into small units. Each student's progress is assessed repeatedly through supervised practice, and learning time is adjusted according to the student's aptitude. Students are not allowed to move on to another unit until they have mastered the previous unit. Assessment is based on criteria that set clear expectations and reduce student anxiety. The opportunity to improve performance while receiving feedback from the instructor boosts the learner's confidence and self-esteem. A 2013 review of the literature found that learning for mastery was associated with large benefits in skills and moderate effects on patient outcomes (Cook et al. 2013).

1.2 Purpose of Higher Education

"Higher education" refers to learning in post-secondary institutions such as universities and colleges. They differ in content, organization, goals, social role, and function. The term "university" refers to "an institution of higher education formally authorized to award advanced degrees in three or more academic disciplines or fields of study" (Denman 2009).

Since the 1990s, higher education has changed in response to social mobility and funding (Altbach et al. 2019). In the past, the costs of higher education were covered by public funds; today they are financed by tuition fees. It is argued that the cuts in public funding were not only to save money but also due to the belief that education is a commodity that must be paid for. As a result, students are likely to demand well-taught programs. Some feel that they are entitled to a degree because they paid for it. Faculty today are under multiple pressures: on the one hand, they are expected to teach in a student-friendly way; on the other, they must prevent lowering standards. Higher education has become a competitive enterprise where students must compete for a place at a top institution. Universities compete for ranking and funding from government or private sources. While competition can promote excellence, it can also contribute to a decline in traditional values (Altbach et al. 2019). This subsection aims to explore the purpose and function of higher education and examine some of its proposed roles.

1.2.1 Goals of Higher Education

The purpose of higher education defies definition. Academics pursue different goals and enjoy a high degree of autonomy. A clear mission statement would therefore run the risk of ignoring the goals of some faculty members (Keohane 1993). Nonetheless, the planning of higher education depends on its perceived purpose. This purpose includes various combinations of exploring the world of knowledge, fostering reflectivity, training the workforce, preparing for a career, and promoting regional development.

1.2.1.1 To Explore the World of Knowledge; Promote Reflectivity; Preserve the Heritage of Civilization

The main task of the university is the search for truth and its application to the improvement of human living conditions. Universities attempt to achieve this goal by combining research and teaching through a company of scholars. The term "company of scholars" implies an exchange of ideas and self-criticism, which in turn implies academic freedom for the expression of ideas. Scholars must also produce new scholars and improve people's lives not only through applied research but also by educating a new generation of citizens and leaders (Keohane 1993).

Teaching aims to impart knowledge. Mariam Webster's Dictionary defines knowledge as "the sum of what is known: the totality of truth, information, and principles ..." Whitehead (1952) argued against teaching crumbs of knowledge without application in life. He advocated teaching a few concepts that the learner can reflect on, relate to other areas of knowledge, and apply in life. Reflectivity is seen as essential to practice (Van Beveren et al. 2018) and refers to two skills. The first is Schon's (Schon 1987) "Reflective Practitioner" ability to apply the cyclical loop of theory guiding experience and experience changing theoretical constructs. The acquisition of this skill depends on students' epistemological beliefs and their tolerance of uncertainty (see Sect. 1.1.3). The second skill is Fonagy's "Reflective Function" (Fonagy and Target 1997) of reflecting on one's thinking/feeling and that of others. As such, it encompasses the concepts of moral reasoning, emotional intelligence, self-awareness, and empathy.

Universities have played an important role in the development of civilization. Their purpose vacillated between satisfying societal needs and those of the individual, thereby restricting the freedom of teaching and learning and losing sight of the overarching goal: the dissemination and advancement of knowledge for the sake of knowledge itself (Denman 2009). It remains uncertain whether state and market forces will compel universities to promote only utilitarian knowledge.

1.2.1.2 To Train Manpower and Prepare for a Career

Higher education institutions are often criticized for not preparing their graduates for the real world. Policymakers have repeatedly called for investment in personal skills. Industry has reinforced this call by demanding that universities train professionals who can meet society's needs. These demands are consistent with Whitehead's shift in emphasis from the transmission of information to its reflective application. Consequently, graduate employability has become one of the issues that define the mission of universities.

A systematic review found that between 2009 and 2019, higher education institutions were more concerned with developing graduates' employability skills than their reflective skills. One of the main problems was the (mis)match between graduates' skills and employers' requirements. This mismatch was less evident in courses leading to a specific profession, such as medicine, engineering, and computer science. Not so in programs such as geography, where it was not clear what graduates would do. Abelha et al. (2020) concluded that graduate employability and skills development require innovation in higher education. However, they found no studies on interventions intended to promote employability in higher education.

1.2.1.3 To Provide New Experiences and Facilitate Learner's Development

In recent decades, efforts have been made to define and operationalize the features of human development. The most studied traits are epistemological development, tolerance of uncertainty, moral reasoning, empathy, emotional intelligence, and the capacity for reflection.

The Perry scale (Perry 1968) and the Reflective Judgment Model by King and Kitchener (2004) are generally used for *epistemological development*. These models describe a sequence of stages that Perry refers to as dualism, multiplicity, relativism, and commitment in relativism. In Dualism, students think in terms of right and wrong and believe that teachers know the right answers. The transition to Multiplicity begins when students encounter conflicting opinions or teachers who respond with "I don't know." Now, students consider multiple opinions legitimate only in areas where the correct answer has not yet been found. In these areas, students believe that "opinions cannot be judged." Towards the end of Multiplicity, students realize that opinions *can* be judged even in areas of uncertainty, as there can be a limited number of solutions to a problem that is congruent with the available data and an unlimited number of illogical approaches. This signals their transition to relativism. Now students would say, "I disagree, but you might be right," rather than "I disagree and therefore you are wrong," as in Dualism. At this stage, students realize that there is no absolute truth. Students reach the stage of Commitment in relativism when they understand that they must commit to a decision if they do not want to remain in indecision, even if they will regret it in the future.

The development of Perry's scheme can be seen as a decline in *intolerance of uncertainty*. Intolerance of uncertainty is the tendency to perceive ambiguous situations as a source of discomfort or threat. Uncertainty was rejected in dualism, seen as temporary in multiplicity, accepted as legitimate in relativism, and dealt with when students affirmed themselves in their commitments. Tolerance of uncertainty has been mostly measured with self-administered instruments (e.g., Hancock and Mattick 2020).

Moral reasoning is measured by asking an individual why certain actions are perceived as just. Its most common measure is the Defining Issues Test (DIT) (Rest 1994). The test distinguishes between three stages of development. The "preconventional" stage is observed in children who define "right" as the avoidance of punishment. The "conventional" stage characterizes adolescents who define actions as right when they are approved by others and conform to social norms. The "postconventional" stage is typified by the adoption of principles that are considered valid beyond social norms. Moral reasoning is an essential component of doctors' professional behavior and is believed to be crucial for medicine and linked to clinical performance and decision-making (Sheehan et al. 1980; Baldwin and Self 2006).

Emotional intelligence refers to the ability to manage one's emotions and understand the feelings of others. It includes five elements: self-awareness, self-regulation, motivation, empathy, and social skills. Self-awareness is knowing one's emotions, strengths, weaknesses, drives, values, and goals and their impact on others. Self-regulation is the ability to control one's feelings and to adapt to changing circumstances. Social skills are managing relationships with others. And motivation is being aware of what motivates others. Emotional intelligence is measured using self-administered instruments. The effort to develop it has mostly emphasized workplace training and career development. It has been suggested that higher education can play an important role in developing emotional intelligence by incorporating various techniques into educational processes, pedagogy, and curricula (Stratton et al. 2008; Chew et al. 2013; Kastberg et al. 2020).

Empathy is variously equated with a cognitive insight into another person's psychological perspective and with an affective response to another person's distress. These different definitions explain the difficulties in measuring empathy. Empathy has been assessed using pencil and paper tests, peer ratings, patient ratings, and observed behaviors.

Studies of the development of these traits during higher education have yielded contradictory results. On the one hand, graduate students have been reported to have higher levels of *epistemological development* than undergraduate students (Jehng et al. 1993; Paulsen and Wells 1998; Wise et al. 2004). Social science and humanities students were more likely to believe that knowledge is uncertain and relied more on their reasoning abilities than engineering and economics students. *Moral reasoning* (DIT) scores have been reported to be related to epistemological beliefs (Bendixen et al. 1998) and to increase during college (King and Mayhew 2002), nursing (Duckett et al. 1997; Wirtz 2007), physical therapy (Geddes et al. 2009), and pharmacy (Gallagher 2011) education.

On the other hand, medical students predominantly espoused simplistic *epistemological thinking* (Knight and Mattick 2006) and their reflective skills deteriorated in their final year of study (Chalmers et al. 2011). Studies comparing junior and senior medical students found either no significant differences (Hancock and Mattick 2020) or a decline (Han et al. 2015) in *tolerance of uncertainty*. Similarly, in contrast to the observed increase in *moral reasoning* scores among college, nursing, physical therapy, and pharmacy students, most authors have not observed such an increase during the undergraduate medical curriculum (Self et al. 1993; Hren et al. 2011; Murrell 2014; Hegazi and Wilson 2013). This seems to confirm the claims of ethical erosion in medical students and that their moral development is inhibited by undergraduate medical education. *Emotional intelligence* scores slightly increase with age (Fariselli et al. 2008) and remain stable in medical students (Stratton et al. 2008; Chew et al. 2013). None of the studies found increasing *empathy* scores during medical training (see Neumann et al. 2011 for a review).

Hegazi and Wilson 2013 suggested two ways of interpreting the absence of increase or decline in epistemological development, tolerance of uncertainty, moral reasoning, empathy, and emotional intelligence in medical students. They could be interpreted as "loss of idealism": junior students, newly admitted to medical school, tend to consider more humanitarian concerns and to disregard self-interest. With time, these students become more pragmatic and less idealistic. Alternatively, it has been suggested that students show a decline in moral development during the process of medical education because of the medical curriculum (overt or hidden).

1.2.1.4 To Improve the Quality of Citizenship and Promote Regional Development

Universities are no longer seen as isolated islands in society. They are expected to play a role in the economic and cultural development of their regions and to tailor their activities to the needs of society. In addition to research and teaching, universities have taken on a third role, namely service. Social scientists consider tasks such as "applied research," "regional development," "innovation," and "outreach" as part of the core activities of universities (Pinheiro et al. 2015).

However, a 2016 review of the literature found mixed evidence that higher education institutions contribute to regional governance, the economy, and "good citizenship." The authors concluded that the relationships between higher education institutions and the region are shaped by the characteristics of the region, the cultural and political conditions, and the study programs offered by the universities (Peer and Penker 2016).

1.3 Institutions of Higher Education

A comprehensive statement describing higher education institutions in general and medical schools in particular should include their context and mission. The institutional context refers to the academic freedom of the faculty (e.g., to pursue personal research interests or institutional and community interests), funding (government, endowments), and the stakeholders to whom it is accountable (learners, patients, the medical profession, health services, the community, and government).

The mission of a higher education institution refers to its goals. The wording of a mission statement is intentionally vague to ensure consistency between different departments (chemistry and statistics; faculty and administration). However, the statement must be clear enough to define their role in achieving the institution's goals. An agreed mission statement is necessary to unify a pluralistic group trying to achieve a common goal. This is especially true for medical schools that include clinicians, researchers, process-oriented administrators, and outcome-oriented professionals.

Despite the unifying value of institutional goals, they are not a practical working tool. They do not define specific teaching programs, such as biochemistry. The implementation of such programs requires their translation into learning objectives that define the expectations from their graduates. The more detailed these are, the more targeted the teaching and the assessment of its outcomes can be. By analogy, travelers in an unfamiliar country need a large-scale map to know where they are going and a detailed topographical map to know how to get there.

Other features of universities and medical schools include, first, information on the design of the curriculum (Chap. 2), its components (pre-clinical and clinical phases), learning environments (classroom or small group learning; skills labs; block clerkship rotations in medical care centers or continuous clerkships in primary care clinics). Second, the requirements for admission of learners and their assessment (paper and pencil examinations, oral examination, global assessments). Third, the expected competencies of the graduate, such as self-directed learning. And finally, the type of pedagogical support (student counseling, evaluation of tests, student ratings of teaching, audiovisual aids).

1.4 Summing up

The transition from the theories of higher education to the reality of curriculum planning and design is a huge leap. The most important question is how to translate the mission of higher education into concrete behavioral objectives. How can a course specification ensure the emergence of individuals who "possess both culture and expertise" (Whitehead 1952), "democracy of mind" (Frye 1971), or a person who can "master any subject with facility" (Kerr 1972)? Evidence shows that the same courses can be delivered differently with similar immediate results. But what about in the long term?

The undergraduate medical curriculum seeks to produce reflective physicians and promote professionalism in learners by including courses in medical ethics. A 2015 analysis of medical ethics education in the United States found that it has become integral to medical education (Carrese et al. 2015). In recent years, it has received particular attention as the Liaison Committee on Medical Education and the Accreditation Council for Graduate Medical Education have emphasized professional education. However, despite the development of standards and competencies related to professionalism, there is no consensus on the specific goals of medical ethics education, the essential knowledge and skills expected from learners, the best pedagogical methods and processes for implementation, and strategies for assessment.

References

Abelha M, Fernandes S, Mesquita D, Seabra F, Ferreira-Oliveira AT. Graduate employability and competence development in higher education—a systematic literature review using PRISMA. Sustainability. 2020;12(15):5900.

Altbach PG, Reisberg L, Rumbley LE. Trends in global higher education: tracking an academic revolution. Leiden: Brill; 2019.

Baldwin DC, Self DJ. The assessment of moral reasoning and professionalism in medical education and practice. In: Measuring medical professionalism. Oxford: Oxford University Press; 2006. p. 75–94.

Benbassat J. Role modeling in medical education: the importance of a reflective imitation. Acad Med. 2014;89(4):550–4.

Bendixen LD, Schraw G, Dunkle ME. Epistemic beliefs and moral reasoning. J Psychol. 1998;132(2):187–200.

Bloom BS. Learning for Mastery. Instruction and curriculum. Regional education Laboratory for the Carolinas and Virginia, topical papers and reprints, number 1. Evaluation Comment. 1968;1:n2. Accessed ED053419.pdf June 2023.

Calman KC, Downie RS. Education and training in medicine. Med Educ. 1988;22:488–91.

Carrese JA, Malek J, Watson K, Lehmann LS, Green MJ, McCullough LB, Geller G, Braddock CH III, Doukas DJ. The essential role of medical ethics education in achieving professionalism: the Romanell report. Acad Med. 2015;90(6):744–52.

Chalmers P, Dunngalvin A, Shorten G. Reflective ability and moral reasoning in final year medical students: a semi-qualitative cohort study. Med Teach. 2011;33:e281–9.

Chew BH, Zain AM, Hassan F. Emotional intelligence and academic performance in the first and final year medical students: a cross-sectional study. BMC Med Educ. 2013;13:44.

Cook DA, Brydges R, Zendejas B, Hamstra SJ, Hatala R. Mastery learning for health professionals using technology-enhanced simulation: a systematic review and meta-analysis. Acad Med. 2013;88(8):1178–86.

Denman BD. What is a university in the 21st century? Higher Educ Manag Policy. 2009;17:9–28.

Duckett L, Rowan M, Ryden M, Krichbaum K, Miller M, Wainwright H, Savik K. Progress in the moral reasoning of baccalaureate nursing students between program entry and exit. Nurs Res. 1997;46:222–9.

Fariselli L, Ghini M, Freedman J. Age, and emotional intelligence. Six Seconds. 2008;22:1. Accessed June 2024. Microsoft Word - WP EQ and Age.doc (researchgate.net).

Fonagy P, Target M. Attachment and reflective function: their role in self-organization. Dev Psychopathol. 1997;9:679–700.

Frye N. The definition of a University in Alternatives in education. Bruce Rusk ed, OISE 5th anniversary lectures. Toronto: General Publishing Co; 1971. p. 71–90.

Gallagher CT. Assessment of levels of moral reasoning in pharmacy students at different stages of the undergraduate curriculum. Int J Pharm Pract. 2011;19:374–80.

Geddes EL, Salvatori P, Eva KW. Does moral judgment improve in occupational therapy and physiotherapy students over the course of their pre-licensure training? Learn Health Soc Care. 2009;8:92–102.

Han PK, Schupack D, Daggett S, Holt CT, Strout TD. Temporal changes in tolerance of uncertainty among medical students: insights from an exploratory study. Med Educ Online. 2015;20:282–5.

Hancock J, Mattick K. Tolerance of ambiguity and psychological Well-being in medical training: a systematic review. Med Educ. 2020;54(2):125–37.

Hegazi I, Wilson I. Medical education and moral segmentation in medical students. Med Educ. 2013;47(10):1022–8.

Hren D, Marusic M, Marusic A. Regression of moral reasoning during medical education: combined design study to evaluate the effect of clinical study years. PLoS One. 2011;6:e17406.

Jehng JCJ, Johnson SD, Anderson RC. Schooling and students' epistemological beliefs about learning. Contemp Educ Psychol. 1993;18:23–35.

Kastberg E, Buchko A, Buchko K. Developing emotional intelligence: the role of higher education. J Organ Psychol. 2020;20(3):1.

Keohane NO. The Mission of the research university. Deadalus. 1993;122:101–25.

Kerr C. The uses of the university. 2nd ed. New York: Harper and Row; 1972.

King PM, Kitchener KS. Reflective judgment: theory and research on the development of epistemic assumptions through adulthood. Educ Psychol. 2004;39:5–18.

King PM, Mayhew MJ. Moral judgment development in higher education: insights from the defining issues test. J Moral Educ. 2002;31:247–70.

Knight LV, Mattick K. 'When I first came here, I thought medicine was black and white': making sense of medical students' ways of knowing. Soc Sci Med. 2006;63:1084–96.

Murrell VS. The failure of medical education to develop moral reasoning in medical students. Int J Med Educ. 2014;5:219–25.

References

Neumann M, Edelhauser F, Tauschel D, Fischer MR, Wirtz M, Woop C. Empathy decline and its reasons: a systematic review of studies with medical students and residents. Acad Med. 2011;86:996–1009.

Paulsen MB, Wells CT. Domain differences in the epistemological beliefs of college students. Res High Educ. 1998;39:365–84.

Peer V, Penker M. Higher education institutions and regional development: a meta-analysis. Int Reg Sci Rev. 2016;39:228–53.

Perry WG. Forms of intellectual and ethical development in the college years. New York: Holt, Reinhart & Winston; 1968.

Peters RS. Ethics and education. London: George Allen and Unwin Ltd.; 1966.

Pinheiro R, Langa PV, Pausits A. One and two equal three? The third mission of higher education institutions. Eur J Higher Educ. 2015;5:233–49.

Rest JR, ed. Moral development in the professions: psychology and applied ethics. Hove: Psychology Press; 1994.

Schon DA. Educating the reflective practitioner. San Francisco: Jossey-Bass; 1987.

Self DJ, Schrader DE, Baldwin DC Jr, Wolinsky FD. The moral development of medical students: a pilot study of the possible influence of medical education. Med Educ. 1993;27(1):26–34.

Sheehan TJ, Husted SD, Candee D, Cook CD, Bargen M. Moral judgment as a predictor of clinical performance. Eval Health Prof. 1980;3(4):393.

Stratton TD, Saunders JA, Elam CL. Changes in medical students' emotional intelligence: an exploratory study. Teach Learn Med. 2008;20:279–84.

Van Beveren L, Roets G, Buysse A, Rutten K. We all reflect, but why? A systematic review of the purposes of reflection in higher education in social and behavioral sciences. Educ Res Rev. 2018;24:1–9.

Whitehead AN. The aim of education and other essays. New York: The New American Library; 1952.

Wirtz EF. The moral integrity development of nursing students in two-year colleges. Bozeman: Montana State University; 2007. Accessed June 2024. Microsoft Word—77027-1177071715-EDCI_690_Front_matter_4_15 (psu.edu).

Wise JC, Lee SH, Litzinger T, Marra RM, Palmer B. A report on a four-year longitudinal study of the intellectual development of engineering undergraduates. J Adult Dev. 2004;11:103–10.

Chapter 2
Curriculum Design

Abstract The definition of the term "curriculum" is controversial. As a rule, this term implies a sequence of learning events designed to achieve educational objectives. The terms curriculum and teaching programs are interchangeably used and refer to a course outline, content, a list of course objectives, and examinations. Other authors argue that a curriculum cannot be reduced to teaching programs alone. They see a curriculum as an outline of a system that includes a description of the curricular process, such as learning activities, teaching materials, the pedagogical system, and a review of students' and teachers' performance. Still, other authors expand the definition of curriculum to include a comprehensive description of the institutional environment, learners, teachers, teaching/learning process, assessment, and pedagogical support. This section further defines these three components of the term curriculum and Chap. 3 explains how each component entails different approaches to curriculum assessment.

2.1 The Curriculum as a Teaching Program

2.1.1 Components of a Teaching Program: Knowledge, Skills, and Attitudes

A teaching program is expected to impart knowledge, skills, and attitudes. *Knowledge* is imparted to learners by lectures, "flipped classrooms" (the teacher asks students to study outside of class and uses class time for specific class activities), and self-study. The advantage of lectures is their low cost. A lecturer with a suitable sound amplification system can impart knowledge to hundreds of students. Lectures fulfill students' expectations by focusing on topics that teachers consider important. The disadvantage of lectures is that they force students to suppress the urge to think about what they hear during the lecture, as this would result in them missing what is said afterward. Furthermore, lectures create a dependency on the teacher as a source of information and do not familiarize students with other sources of knowledge that they will hopefully use in the future.

Therefore, the approach of innovative medical schools (Chap. 4) is to encourage students to acquire knowledge through self-study. Instead of preparing lectures, teachers would spend their time clarifying the learning objectives and preparing exams to assess whether these objectives have been met. Students would study alone and meet with teachers to clear up issues they did not understand. The disadvantage of self-study is that it requires personal discipline from the students and a system of assignments and monitoring from the medical school.

Skills refer to actions that the student must be able to perform and their level of performance (knowing about them; having watched someone perform them; having performed them under supervision; being able to perform them unsupervised; and being able to teach them). Teaching skills include motivation (explaining the nature of the skill and its importance), demonstration, and supervised practice. Explanations and demonstrations can be given to groups of students. Supervised practice requires personal mentoring and advanced simulations of clinical problems, like airplane pilot training (Cook et al. 2013).

The emphasis on teaching skills in clinical settings and skills laboratories is relatively new in medical education. Until the 1970s, it was assumed that students would acquire skills informally and through casual observation during clinical clerkships. The need for supervised practice became apparent in the 1970s when repeated observations of physicians revealed deficits in patient interviewing (Platt and McMath 1979; Beckman and Frankel 1984) and even in understanding patient complaints (Freidin et al. 1990).

Contrary to popular belief, I do not believe that personal example is the preferred way to teach *attitudes and values* to medical students because no medical school always has perfect teachers. We all have shortcomings and may behave incorrectly when upset, tired, or anxious. Therefore, the purpose of teaching attitudes is to curb the natural tendency of medical students to imitate their teachers. The first step in teaching values is to make students aware that there will always be a gap between the ideal and the reality, and that although this gap is inevitable, it can be narrowed. I suggest teaching appropriate attitudes and values through small group discussions about specific adverse events, such as rude treatment of patients, medical errors, and demanding payment for services included in the insurance basket. Ignoring these issues can lead to embarrassment and cynicism; discussing them can lead to effective coping and an awareness that none of us is immune from inappropriate behavior or errors in judgment.

2.1.2 Structure of a Teaching Program: Prerequisites

The undergraduate medical curriculum consists of a sequence of steps. Each step prepares the learner for the next and can be seen as a "client" of the previous step. For example, knowledge of pre-clinical sciences is a prerequisite for the clinical clerkship because it familiarizes students with the terminology necessary to communicate with other healthcare providers, as well as the structure and function of the human body in health (anatomy, physiology) and disease (pathology, pathophysiology, pharmacology, and bacteriology). Skills required include performing a patient interview and physical examination, accessing information, drawing venous blood, and administering intramuscular and subcutaneous injections. The clerkships shift their focus from "What does the student know?" to "What can the student do?" This requires a change in the definition of the role of clinical tutors from a source of knowledge to supervisors of student performance. Completing the clinical clerkships is in turn a prerequisite for residency.

Opinions differ as to whether the prerequisites for the clerkship should include, first, knowledge of statistics, epidemiology, medical sociology, medical ethics and familiarity with terms such as case-control study, sensitivity and specificity of tests and bias and, second, an understanding of the terminology and methods of inquiry that define the various scientific disciplines as such.

2.1.3 Structure of a Teaching Program: Learning Objectives

"Would you tell me please, which way I ought to go from here?"
"That depends a good deal on where you want to go," said the Cat.
"I don't much care where ___," said Alice.
"Then it doesn't matter which way you go," said the Cat.
"___ so long as I get somewhere," Alice added as an explanation.
"Oh, you are sure to do that," said the Cat, "if you only walk long enough" (Lewis Carrol, Alice in Wonderland).

It is widely agreed that everything we do is a means to an end and that the "end" determines the means to achieve it. In the case of education, the "end" is its outcome. In 1949, Tyler suggested that a curriculum statement should answer the questions: What are the school's aims? What experiences are likely to achieve these goals? How can these experiences be organized? How can one determine if the goals are being achieved? (Tyler 2011).

Tyler's "outcome-based" or "aptitude-based" curriculum is guided by its objectives. The phrase "learning objectives" refers to the observable behaviors that indicate learning success. Setting learning objectives helps to decide how they would be achieved and how their achievement is ascertained. It has been argued that a teacher who provides students with a copy of the learning objectives may not need to teach (Stenhouse and Verma 1981).

Although Tyler's work is highly influential, the need for explicit learning objectives is controversial. Opponents claim that a knowledge syllabus may be perceived as permission not to know what it does not include, that it could limit the teacher's academic freedom, and that there is no limit to the learning opportunities offered by the clinical clerkships. Proponents of defining learning objectives claim that a lack of information about what students are supposed to learn can paralyze their learning; that "you need to know everything" is equivalent to "you don't need to know anything"; that in the absence of a list of objectives, instructors can emphasize rare and exotic topics that interest them; that the explosion of information no longer makes it possible to know everything; and that one of the challenges for members of medical school teaching committees is to define the boundary between the knowledge and skills required of medical students and those required of residents.

For example, by the end of the clerkship, students are expected to formulate a patient's problem list, summarize his/her history and findings, propose a differential diagnosis, design a sensible management plan, and inform the patient about his/her illness. The clinical clerkship cannot prepare a medical student for all possible situations. Therefore, its main objective is to impart an ability to deal with unfamiliar clinical problems. This includes, first, structuring a problem and identifying the data needed to solve it, second, retrieving the data from databases in real-time, third, using decision support systems, and fourth, seeking help from other medical and paramedical professionals or referring the patient to other healthcare providers.

Today, however, the hospital-based block clerkship rotations rarely challenge students to resolve a diagnostic problem, as most patients they see are already diagnosed. The claim that clinical problem-solving can be taught by observing role models is as absurd as the contention that a surgeon can learn to operate only by observing other surgeons.

2.2 The Curriculum as a Process

The main disadvantage of Tyler's outcome-based model is the restriction of its objectives to knowledge and skills (Stenhouse and Verma 1981). As explained in Chap. 3, it focuses on achieving only short-term educational goals that are easy to define; goals that are more difficult to assess may disappear from teachers' minds and the curriculum. Furthermore, outcome assessment is global. It can only be conducted after the completion of the curriculum, but not before its implementation; and in the case of an undesirable outcome, outcome-based assessment cannot determine what went wrong in the implementation of the curriculum.

These limitations have led to a curriculum focused on the teaching process rather than the product. In a sense, the "process model" is the opposite of the aptitude model. The process model views a curriculum as a value in and of itself and not a means to an end. It looks at its need, logic, relevance, appropriateness of its approach, feasibility, cost-effectiveness, and acceptability by students and teachers. The outcome evaluation attempts to answer the question: Has the curriculum achieved its objectives? The process evaluation attempts to answer the question: Is it likely that the curriculum will achieve its objectives? This question has raised the distinction between student-centered, teacher-centered, and developmental curriculum models.

2.2.1 Student-Centered Vs Teacher-Centered Models

> The principal function of education is to transmit the culture - to enable new members of a group to profit from what others have already learned. It follows that the principal task of the student is to learn what others already know (Skinner 1974).

> I see the facilitation of learning as the aim of education, how we develop the learning man, how we can learn to live as individuals in the process. I see the facilitation of learning as the function which may hold constructive, tentative, changing, process answers to some of the deepest perplexities which beset man today (Rogers, as quoted by Zimring 1994).

These opposing views have influenced curricula at all levels of education. Skinner's position inevitably leads to a teacher-centered (didactic) design: a design that views the teacher as the authority who determines what is learned and how it is learned. The students receive knowledge through lectures and learn skills by imitating role models. On the other hand, Rogers sees the teacher as a facilitator who is subordinate to the student's learning needs. Learner-centered programs give students the freedom and responsibility to direct their learning. This approach views the tutor's role not to teach, but to ensure that all students participate in discussions and share their knowledge with the other students in the group. Strict learner-centered programs assume that tutors do not need content knowledge if they can guide students' discussions, and even if they have this knowledge, they should not pass it on to the students (Savery 2006). The design of these curricular models raises the following questions.

Is it necessary to design a curriculum that is either teacher-centered or learner-centered, but never both? The "teacher-centered" and "learner-centered" approaches are not mutually exclusive. Rather, they can be seen as a continuum. One example of this is the teaching of patient interviewing. On the one hand, students are reported to feel uncomfortable with a teacher-centered approach to patient interviewing (Rees et al. 2002). On the other hand, it would be unreasonable to expect students to discover patient interviewing skills without guidance. Therefore, patient interviewing instruction requires an integrated learner- and teacher-centered approach, also described as case-based and inquiry learning (Srinivasan et al. 2007).

Like the teacher-centered strategy, the integrated approach is guided by specific learning objectives. The tutor attempts to achieve these objectives by providing students with information, demonstrating appropriate skills, and supervising students as they practice these skills. As with the learner-centered strategy, the tutor avoids an authoritarian attitude toward the students and encourages them to acquire knowledge through discussion. The tutor should moderate these discussions, gain insights into the learners' familiarity with the topic, and help them build on this knowledge.

In contrast to the teacher-centered approach, which consists of lectures with minimal learner participation, and unlike the learner-centered approach, which is limited to self-directed learning, the integrated approach encourages constant dialog between the tutor and the learners. In contrast to strictly learner-centered programs, where teachers are only expected to facilitate small group discussions, teachers in the integrated approach are expected to master the subject matter and facilitate the exchange of ideas.

The integrated approach is in line with modern adult learning theories. Adults are motivated by learning that builds on their previous experiences (Brookfield 1988). They learn more effectively when, first, they are self-motivated rather than reacting to the demands of others; second, they use experiential techniques such as discussion or problem-solving rather than listening to lectures; third, they derive their learning needs from real-life problems; and fourth, they are challenged to apply the skills or knowledge they acquire to their circumstances (Knowles 1990). There is evidence that an integrated approach is more effective than a purely learner-centered approach. Students and faculty at two academic medical centers overwhelmingly preferred case-based learning over problem-based learning (Srinivasan et al. 2007). Comparative studies between small groups led by tutors without subject matter expertise (i.e., a purely learner-centered approach) and tutors who were both subject matter experts and facilitators (i.e., an integrated approach) showed that the latter tended to take a more direct role in tutorials, speak more frequently and for longer periods, provide more direct answers to students' questions, and suggest more topics for discussion. Students tutored by subject experts reportedly spent more time on self-study and performed better in examinations than students tutored by non-expert tutors (see Schmidt et al. 1987 for a review).

Should didactic methods be the subject of institutional policy? Since the 1970s, medical schools have replaced traditional teacher-centered instruction with learner-centered methods, such as flipped classrooms and problem-based learning. Some schools have adopted learner-centered methods as institutional policy. However, I feel that mandating a single didactic approach limits teachers' freedom to choose the approach with which they feel most comfortable, and different subjects require different teaching strategies.

For example, students seem to be interested in lectures that summarize clinical knowledge, and both learners and teachers would benefit from the opportunity to convey a thesis in the form of a lecture, as is common in scientific meetings. However, while students find lectures on patient interviewing as unneeded sermons in essential politeness, they eagerly discuss the topic when asked to name patient complaints (e.g., "the doctor was rude," ".... did not listen," "… did not understand"). In the specific area of patient interviewing, the integrated teaching approach seems to be more effective than lectures and even the only way to teach (Benbassat and Baumal 2001).

Therefore, I believe that rather than prescribing a particular didactic approach, faculty should familiarize themselves with alternative teaching methods, such as live or video lectures, flipped classrooms, problem-based learning, and an integrated teaching approach. Teachers would be encouraged to evaluate the effectiveness of different teaching methods for diverse subjects and should choose the didactic methods they consider optimal to stimulate students' interest.

2.2.2 Matching and Developmental Models

Curriculum models that fail to articulate the relationships between learner characteristics and instructional interventions leave gaping holes in their design. The matching model views the achievement of educational goals as a function of the interaction between learners, teachers, and the classroom environment. It assumes that there are individual differences in learners' responses to different parts of their learning environment. The task of curriculum design is to identify these individual differences and provide appropriate teaching interventions that correspond to these differences. However, although logical, this view says nothing about the nature of these teaching interventions, and most authorities who originally endorsed the matching model later seem to lose faith in it. The interactions between learner variables and the classroom environment are difficult to define and quantify. Despite the disappointment with the matching model, it is worth examining why a model with such obvious face validity could not fulfill its original promise.

The development model brings an additional dimension to the matching model. Whereas the matching model assumes that learners have stable characteristics such as motivation, perception, and understanding, the developmental model assumes that people mature in their cognitive, emotional, and ethical development (see Sect. 1.1.3). Therefore, the developmental model is dynamic; it anticipates changes in learners' stages and adapts curriculum interventions accordingly.

To expect a university teacher to adapt to the differences between individual learners and their stages of development is, in my opinion, too much and too costly. However, this expectation is likely to be met by online learning which gives learners control over the content, sequence, and pace of learning and thus promotes individualized (adaptive) learning (Papapanou et al. 2022).

2.3 The Curriculum as an All-Inclusive Statement

The disadvantages of a curriculum based on process alone led Stufflebeam (2000) to propose his context, input, process, and product (CIPP) model.

2.3.1 Context

"Context" identifies educational needs and provides a rationale for learning objectives. Boerhaave is credited with being the first to discern between the pre-medical, pre-clinical, and clinical components of medical education and to introduce clinical teaching in academic hospitals in the eighteenth century. Since then, medicine has been considered a profession with a scientific base. A solid knowledge of science is thought to be essential for clinical medicine.

In the 1950s, teaching was based on the biomedical model of clinical medicine. It focused on the etiology and pathogenesis of diseases. Knowledge was deterministic (right/wrong), with causes leading inevitably to their effects rather than through probabilities. Treatment decisions and prognoses remained in the sphere of medical art and intuition. Biomedical sciences were assumed to provide learners with a framework of knowledge within which to understand and consider causal relationships between phenomena, and a structure for unstructured problems. Today, however, evidence that psychosocial risk indicators are more closely linked to disease than biomedical factors has led to the inclusion of the social and behavioral sciences in medical curricula. The bio-psycho-social model of clinical practice replaced the biomedical model. We no longer refer to etiology but to risk indicators of disease, and deterministic right-wrong thinking is substituted by stochastic reasoning.

2.3.2 Input

"Input" refers to work plans, budgets, and resources for implementing the curriculum. Since the 1950s, the medical school has functioned as a holding company for preclinical and clinical departments. The departments value their teaching commitments because they bring prestige and additional posts. Faculty are encouraged to initiate discussions on medical education and workshops on improving teaching, medical ethics, and the history of medicine. However, teaching is given a lower priority than patient care and research. Applicants are still selected for admission to medical school if they have proven their ability to learn and are judged to be well-rounded individuals by various tests. Once admitted, medical students are the raw material that faculty mold into competent professionals.

In the 1950s, department chairs determined teaching policy, objectives, methods, assessment, and budget allocations. Basic scientists and clinical instructors held positions because of their expertise, not their teaching skills. The conventional wisdom was that a subject matter expert would be a better teacher than an expert in teaching methods. Some faculty members were permitted to experiment with innovative teaching methods if they did not provoke student criticism and were not associated with deterioration in student performance in examinations.

Today, teaching remains the responsibility of the faculty. However, many, if not most, medical schools have various units or departments that support education (see Sect. 4.1). Tuition fees replaced public funding for higher education thus raising student expectations from the "process" of teaching.

2.3.3 Process

"Process" relates to educational activities. In the 1950s, teaching was content-oriented and teacher-centered. Teachers controlled what was to be learned, how, and when. The lessons mainly took the form of lectures. Students were passive recipients of knowledge and were treated without stratification according to interest, ability, or prior knowledge. They were expected to take notes during lectures and read them to prepare for the exams. Training for clinical skills was unsystematic, by casual observation during the clerkship rotations and as recently as the 2010s, medical school graduates were claimed to have inadequate skills in teamwork, information management (Crosson et al. 2011), and basic surgical procedures (Mattar et al. 2013).

Consequently, medical schools emphasize today competency-based education that focuses on what students can do rather than what they know (Ryan et al. 2022). Unsystematic learning of clinical skills has evolved into supervised training and hands-on practice using simulated and real patients. Bladder drainage, emergency interventions, blood sampling, and resuscitation are taught in skills labs using simulators. Anatomy courses teach students how to interpret imaging studies, and virtual patients are used to address specific clinical encounters. Students must demonstrate that they have achieved a certain level of performance before being admitted to the clerkships. Aside from its contribution to patient safety, simulation-based teaching appears superior to traditional clinical education in skill acquisition. It is associated with better patient outcomes than no intervention and non-simulation-based teaching (Zendejas et al. 2013).

Today, medical educators accept that learners may progress at different rates and recommend providing them with learning goals and allowing students to self-direct their learning rather than requiring them to spend a predefined period on a unit of study (Frank et al. 2010). Teaching focuses on information retrieval skills and clinical reasoning. The emphasis is no longer on memorization but on self-directed learning and the ability to retrieve information using advanced information technology, smartphone applications, and e-learning. Instead of lecturing, instructors increasingly ask their students to learn out of class. The COVID-19 pandemic further promoted distance learning, e-learning, novel student assessment methods, and Zoom instruction (Rose 2020).

Online learning does not differ in effectiveness from traditional education (Papapanou et al. 2022). It is more cost-effective than classroom learning as individuals from different institutions can participate in courses; it generates higher student satisfaction rates (He et al. 2021); it provides learners with control over the content, sequence, and pace of learning thereby promoting individualized (adaptive) learning. The barriers to the implementation of online teaching are inadequate infrastructure, lack of institutional policies and support, and negative attitudes among stakeholders (O'Doherty et al. 2018).

In the 1950s, it was assumed that if students learn the content well enough, problem-solving will come naturally with experience and exposure to the right role model. Although recognized as necessary, self-directed learning was considered inefficient and time-consuming, leading to the acquisition of faulty habits and skills. It was believed that early exposure of students to clinical problems can lead to an unacceptable level of anxiety in students. On the other hand, today, students are exposed to patients from the beginning of their studies. Most countries have sought to improve the quality of their medical schools' teaching programs through periodic external reviews of the extent they meet accreditation standards. Today, the need to learn about all clinical areas is still recognized. However, to achieve this, 6–12 months rounds in a single community clinic are increasingly replacing the block clerkship rotations in tertiary medical centers.

2.3.4 Product

"Product" examines how successful the program is in meeting educational needs. In the 1950s, the graduate was expected to be capable of unsupervised primary patient care backed by consultants and to be ready for any career in clinical medicine or academic research, which would require further studies at a graduate level. Today, it is acknowledged that medicine is an expanding field with increasing amounts of available biomedical knowledge. Single clinicians can no longer provide adequate care. Therefore, rational practice necessitates teamwork and specialization. Medical schools are expected to expose students to all medical specialties so that they can make an informed choice of specialization, including primary care.

References

Beckman HB, Frankel RM. The effect of physician behavior on the collection of data. Ann Intern Med. 1984;101:692–6.
Benbassat J, Baumal R. Teaching doctor-patient interviewing skills using an integrated learner and teacher-centered approach. Am J Med Sci. 2001;322:349–57.
Brookfield SD. Understanding and facilitating adult learning. London: Jossey-Bass Publishers; 1988. p. 9–11.
Cook DA, Hamstra SJ, Brydges R, Zendejas B, Szostek JH, Wang AT, Erwin PJ, Hatala R. Comparative effectiveness of instructional design features in simulation-based education: systematic review and meta-analysis. Med Teach. 2013;35:e867–98.
Crosson FJ, Leu J, Roemer BM, Ross MN. Gaps in residency training should be addressed to better prepare doctors for a twenty-first-century delivery system. Health Aff (Millwood). 2011;30:2142–8.
Frank JR, Snell LS, Cate OT, Holmboe ES, Carraccio C, Swing SR, Harris P, Glasgow NJ, Campbell C, Dath D, Harden RM. Competency-based medical education: theory to practice. Med Teach. 2010;32:638–45.
Freidin RB, Goldman L, Cecil RR. Patient-physician concordance in problem identification in the primary care setting. Ann Intern Med. 1990;93:490–3.
He L, Yang N, Xu L, Ping F, Li W, Sun Q, Li Y, Zhu H, Zhang H. Synchronous distance education vs traditional education for health science students: a systematic review and meta-analysis. Med Educ. 2021;55:293–308.
Knowles M. The adult learner: a neglected species. Houston, Texas: Gulf Publishing; 1990.
Mattar SG, Alseidi AA, Jones DB, Jeyarajah DR, Swanstrom LL, Aye RW, Wexner SD, Martinez JM, Ross SB, Awad MM. General surgery residency inadequately prepares trainees for fellowship: results of a survey of fellowship program directors. Ann Surg. 2013;258:440–9.
O'Doherty D, Dromey M, Lougheed J, Hannigan A, Last J, McGrath D. Barriers and solutions to online learning in medical education–an integrative review. BMC Med Educ. 2018;8:1.

References

Papapanou M, Routsi E, Tsamakis K, Fotis L, Marinos G, Lidoriki I, Karamanou M, Papaioannou TG, Tsiptsios D, Smyrnis N, Rizos E. Medical education challenges and innovations during COVID-19 pandemic. Postgrad Med J. 2022;98:321–7.

Platt FW, McMath JC. Clinical hypo competence: the interview. Ann Intern Med. 1979;91:898–902.

Rees CE, Sheard CE, McPherson AC. A qualitative study to explore undergraduate medical students' attitudes toward interviewing skills learning. Med Teach. 2002;24:289–93.

Rose S. Medical student education in the time of COVID-19. JAMA. 2020;323:2131–2.

Ryan MS, Blood AD, Park YS, Farnan JM. Competency-based frameworks in medical school education programs: a thematic analysis of the academic medicine snapshots, 2020. Acad Med. 2022;97(11S):S63–70.

Savery JR. Overview of problem-based learning: definitions and distinctions. Interdiscip J Probl Based Learn. 2006;1:9–20.

Schmidt HG, Dauphinee WD, Patel VL. Comparing the effects of problem-based and conventional curricula in an international sample. J Med Educ. 1987;62:305–15.

Skinner BF. Designing higher education. Deadalus. 1974;103:196–202.

Srinivasan M, Wilkes M, Stevenson F, Nguyen T, Slavin S. Comparing problem-based learning with case-based learning: effects of a major curricular shift at two institutions. Acad Med. 2007;82:74–82.

Stenhouse L, Verma GK. Educational procedures and attitudinal objectives: a paradox. J Curric Stud. 1981;13(4):329–37.

Stufflebeam DL. The CIPP model for evaluation. In: Evaluation models: viewpoints on educational and human services evaluation. Dordrecht: Springer; 2000. p. 279–317. cipp-model 2003.pdf (uw.edu.pl). Accessed Oct 2023.

Tyler RW. Desirable content for a curriculum development syllabus today. Listening to and learning from students: possibilities for teaching, learning, and curriculum. IAP; 2011. p. 179.

Zendejas B, Brydges R, Wang AT, Cook DA. Patient outcomes in simulation-based medical education: a systematic review. J Gen Intern Med. 2013;28:1078–89.

Zimring F. CARL ROGERS (1902–1987). Prospects: the quarterly review of comparative education, vol. XXIV. Paris: UNESCO: International Bureau of Education; 1994. p. 411–22. https://www.turningpoint.ie/wp-content/uploads/2015/09/About-Carl-Rodgers.pdf. Accessed July 2014.

Chapter 3
The Evaluation of the Medical Curriculum

Abstract Any system that works without feedback is doomed to failure. Curriculum evaluation examines the extent to which an educational program is consistent with its objective. Such an evaluation can be seen as a closed loop. It begins with an assessment of the *need for the curriculum*. This need defines the *learning objectives* that determine the process.

The *process evaluation* examines whether the curriculum is *likely* to attain its objectives including those that are difficult (problem-solving), or impossible (ethical and moral decision-making) to measure by formal examinations; whether students and faculty accept the program objectives, and whether the program's content and methods are relevant, feasible, cost-effective, and consistent with the priorities of the faculty. Commonly used means of process evaluation are students' ratings of instruction, student debriefing, student perception of their learning environment, teachers' debriefing, and curriculum mapping. Finally, e*xaminations* assess whether the objectives were met. Unmet objectives and developments in biomedical knowledge and technology redefine the need for the curriculum.

This section outlines the models of curriculum evaluation and the principles that guide this evaluation.

3.1 The Need for Curriculum Evaluation

The various definitions of the term curriculum may refer to the intended program or the one taught. Curriculum evaluation attempts to overcome this ambiguity by analyzing the degree to which an educational program's content, process, and end-product (outcome) are consistent with its purpose. Such analyses provide feedback and inform decisions to continue, change, or stop the program. A system that works without feedback is bound to malfunction and a learning objective that is not repeatedly evaluated may disappear from faculty awareness.

Regular assessment of the medical curriculum is warranted for several reasons. First, clinical faculty with no training in teaching need to be evaluated on their function more than others. Second, teaching in institutions distant from the parent university necessitates some oversight to ensure an agreed-upon core. Third, effective assessment increases the likelihood that changes in the curriculum will go in the desired direction. Fourth, regular assessments of an educational program and the examinations remind faculty of the direction they should be working toward and help them stay on track. Finally, the curriculum requires overcoming problems from the teacher's perspective. The emphasis on research productivity as a criterion for academic promotion and tenure leads to a corresponding neglect of teaching. Teaching is seen as a thankless, time-consuming, and emotionally draining task. The dean's office is often caught between the need to improve teaching and the reluctance of department heads. One strategy for pressuring faculty to devote more teaching resources is to refer to "external" accreditation standards. When pressure for educational reform comes from the dean's office, a confrontation between deans and faculty ensues. External pressure unites deans and faculty in a common goal.

3.2 Models of Evaluation of Medical Curricula

A curriculum evaluation may be seen as a closed loop. The point of entry into this loop is an assessment of the need(s) for the curriculum. This need defines its learning objectives that define its process. The process includes examinations of the attainment of the learning objectives by the students and objectives that were not achieved redefine the needs of the curriculum.

3.2.1 Evaluation of the Need for the Curriculum

A 2019 scoping review entitled "Do we need a core curriculum for medical students?" highlighted the heterogeneity of the undergraduate curricular designs in UK medical schools (Sharma et al. 2019). The authors recommended designing core curricula and including minimum standards on knowledge and skills for medical students. Adopting and assessing unified standards would reduce variability across medical schools for generic and specialty-specific competencies and ensure that medical schools develop and implement curricula to enable graduates to practice safely and competently.

This recommendation is also valid for medical schools outside the UK. I know of no unified or standardized undergraduate medical curriculum in other countries. Furthermore, medical schools should continuously respond to changes in clinical practice, keeping the curriculum in context and ensuring that students are not overburdened by content. Therefore, the assessment of the need for a core undergraduate curriculum should be updated periodically.

3.2.2 End-Product Evaluation

The end-product (outcome, means-end) evaluation measures the extent to which the educational goals of a program have been achieved. As such, end-product evaluation is logical: a poor outcome discredits any educational program; outcome evaluation is a by-product of student evaluation for promotion purposes; and it reminds faculty to formulate learning objectives and use them as criteria for student evaluation. Medical schools aim to produce graduates who can use communication, knowledge, technical skills, clinical reasoning, emotions, values, and reflection in daily practice (Epstein and Hundert 2002). This diverse taxonomy requires a combination of assessment methods. The most common methods of outcome assessment are examinations. Some authors have assessed the outcome by "client courses," patient ratings, and graduate performance in practice.

Examinations include multiple-choice questions, essays, and oral exams. Written exams that are criterion-referenced and properly evaluated are a reliable measure of knowledge. Oral exams supplement knowledge retention and assess clinical competence by observing student performance on long and short cases, objective structured clinical examinations, and standardized patients (Wass et al. 2001). However, they are expensive regarding faculty time and are limited by low reliability.

The main limitation of internal (medical school) examinations is the frequent use of norm-referenced scales. The main disadvantage of external criterion-referenced examinations (NBME in the USA or LMCC in Canada) is that they promote competition between medical schools in knowledge acquisition and neglect the other components of medical competence. Indeed, a 2002 literature review concluded that current examination formats reliably test knowledge but not important areas of medical practice, such as lifelong learning and professionalism. The authors recommended developing new exam formats that assess clinical reasoning, ambiguity management, professionalism, time management, learning strategies, and teamwork (Epstein and Hundert 2002). Still, present medical school examinations have some validity. They predict performance in the internship and clinical practice (Terry et al. 2017; Hecker et al. 2020). Patients treated by board-certified cardiologists (Norcini et al. 2000) and anesthesiologists (Silber et al. 2002) have better outcomes than patients treated by non-certified care providers.

Another form of end-product assessment of a teaching program is an *evaluation by "client courses."* Medical education consists of a succession of teaching programs, each of which may be viewed as a "client" to the previous one and a prerequisite for the next. Rotem et al. (1983) proposed a framework for assessing teaching programs by analyzing deficiencies in learning, i.e., gaps between what students know and what the teachers expect students to have learned previously. For example, clinical teachers may expect students to have learned in a previous course the physiology of absorption but find students' learning deficient in this area with the resulting difficulties in understanding the pathogenesis of diarrhea. This deficiency may be detected by a pretest, or a general impression obtained during the clerkship rotations and lead to the negotiation of a more effective teaching of the required subject. The proposal by Rotem et al. can help teachers determine the prerequisites of student knowledge and skills needed for starting their courses and identify areas requiring remedial work. This increases collaboration among disciplines, ideally leading to a consensus on objectives, teaching, and evaluation procedures.

Patient ratings provide an inexpensive evaluation of students' communication skills (Wilkinson and Fontaine 2002; Price et al. 2008). Its main limitation is that patients are prone to give highly positive ratings (Korsh and Negrete 1972). Simulated patients can provide clinically meaningful assessment scores and may be more useful for the evaluation (Wright et al. 2014). The number of ratings by simulated patients needed to evaluate students' communication skills is yet to be determined.

Evaluations of graduate performance in the practice setting have been solicited from the graduates themselves and their preceptors in residency programs (Clack 1994; Jones et al. 2002). A 1983 study revealed that most Aberdeen medical graduates thought the curriculum had satisfactorily prepared them for their careers. However, they felt that general practice was under-represented (Richardson 1983). A 1995 survey of UK graduates found that over 70% thought their education had satisfactorily equipped them for practice. However, they identified deficiencies in training for clinical, analytical, communication, management, and technical skills (Clack 1994). A 2005 Dutch study found that the graduates appeared satisfied with their knowledge and skills; and that problem-based learning provided better preparation on several competencies (Prince et al. 2005). A 2012 review suggested that graduates perceived themselves as *least* prepared in acute care (Tallentire et al. 2012). Another 2012 survey of medical school graduates found that the overall mean preparedness score was 3.5 on a five-point scale. Graduates felt most prepared for working with patients and colleagues, history taking, and physical examination. They felt least prepared for prescribing and performing complex practical procedures (Morrow et al. 2012).

3.2.3 Process Evaluation

Despite its logic and low cost, end-product evaluation has limitations. First, it requires the definition of learning objectives. Second, it is easy to measure skills and knowledge retention; however, it is difficult to assess clinical judgment, problem-solving, decision-making, and cost awareness, and it is impossible to measure sensitivity to the patient, ethical and moral decision-making, ability to be a life-long self-directed learner, or motivation to serve the community. Therefore, relying solely on outcome evaluation may result in assessing only short-term goals. Difficulties in follow-up preclude long-term longitudinal evaluation. Third, outcome evaluation provides a global assessment rather than specific feedback on the various components of the curriculum. In cases of an unsatisfactory outcome, such evaluation cannot identify what specifically went wrong.

Hence there is a need for process evaluation. It explores whether the curriculum is *likely* to achieve its goals; whether students and faculty accept the program objectives; and whether the program's content and methods are relevant, feasible, and cost-effective (Stenhouse 1971). Commonly used means of process evaluation are students' ratings of instruction, student debriefing, student perception of their learning environment, teachers' debriefing, and curriculum mapping.

Student ratings of instruction are the main and, in many medical schools, the only measure of teaching effectiveness (Berk 2013). Studies of their reliability, validity, and usefulness have indicated that they are a reliable measure of student satisfaction with a given program, and it stands to reason that a satisfied student is more likely to be a receptive and motivated learner. However, attempts to confirm the validity of student ratings by correlations with various measures of learning have yielded conflicting results (see also Chaps. 4 and 6). On the one hand, some studies found that students' ratings are associated with several indicators of teaching effectiveness: student learning, student comments, alumni ratings, and ratings of teaching by outside observers (Kulik 2001). Students' ratings have been reported to discern between individual teachers (Boerboom et al. 2012) and improve teaching courses (Goldfarb and Morrison 2014). On the other hand, a 2009 meta-analysis found a small, statistically non-significant positive correlation between student learning and ratings. Ten studies found a negative association, and 32 found a positive association (Clayson 2009).

Furthermore, it has been found that students' ratings may be influenced by factors unrelated to teaching effectiveness, such as course workload (Donnon et al. 2010), student motivation for taking the course, anticipated success in examinations (Svanum and Aigner 2011), gender, and interest in the course content (Schiekirka and Raupach 2015). Consequently, the validity of student satisfaction as a measure of teaching effectiveness remains controversial (Svanum and Aigner 2011; Peters et al. 2010; Kulik 2001). Some authors have even claimed that "the … practice of using student evaluations … to determine decisions for retention, promotion, and pay for faculty members is improper and … could be argued to be illegal" (Hornstein 2017).

Learning alone, however, is not the only goal of education. Curricula are expected to foster student cognitive development. Students at different levels of development may perceive differently the quality of teaching. It may be therefore concluded that although student ratings cannot be ignored, they fall short of a complete evaluation of a teaching program, and other measures should be used in conjunction with student ratings to assess teaching effectiveness (Berk 2013).

Debriefing of students and teachers primarily assesses the learning environment. Students' perception of the learning environment, also referred to as the "implicit curriculum," "hidden curriculum," "learning atmosphere," or the school's "ethos," has been studied by focus groups or questionnaires, which solicit information on students' relationship with peers and on the degree of flexibility (or authoritarianism) of faculty, and the emotional climate of the learning setting (Pololi et al. 2017;

Chan et al. 2018). Its positive perception is associated with reduced student burnout (Dyrbye et al. 2009), better learning (Wayne et al. 2013), quality of life, resilience, preparedness for practice, and well-being (Tackett et al. 2017; Chan et al. 2018; Helou et al. 2019). Faculty support of students and faculty success in coping with student anxiety are probably the most important components of the learning environment. The best support students could receive is the realization that their clinical instructors share their difficulties. This, however, would require open, candid behavior, which is incompatible with the normative clinical role model of authoritarian self-assurance.

Curriculum mapping shows the relationships between the curriculum components (Harden 2001). As such, it is a cornerstone to attaining its objectives. Curriculum mapping explains when, how, and what is taught and how it is assessed (Al-Eyd et al. 2018). Its methods consist of identifying the elements of the curriculum and how they are linked. These elements include learning expectations (intended institutional, program, course, and session learning outcomes), learning events (courses' credit units, sessions, instructors, and reading assignments), and instructional and assessment methods (Al-Eyd et al. 2018). Additional aims of curriculum mapping are first, to seek discrepancies between the intended and implemented curricula (Plaza et al. 2007); focus on curricular process elements, such as promoting empathy, that are difficult to measure; match content to the outcome to inform faculty about gaps and redundancies; and review of students' examinations.

Review of curriculum content. Over the past few decades, the needs of adult learners have been studied scientifically. The importance of specific, content-based knowledge is supported by evidence that adults are oriented towards learning needs created by real-world problems and are "performance-oriented" in that they want to apply the skills or knowledge they have acquired to their circumstances (Knowles 1990). Furthermore, evidence suggests that expertise consists of a large knowledge base of domain-specific patterns; of recognition of situations in which these patterns apply; and of reasoning from such recognition to a solution (Perkins and Salomon 1989). However, the existence of general cognitive skills is supported by their application by experts to unfamiliar problems and by evidence that medical and psychology students can transfer probabilistic thinking to everyday problems. Consequently, modern pedagogical approaches call for a synthesis between generality and context specificity in teaching, with general cognitive skills not replacing domain-specific knowledge but rather serving as tools for assimilating that knowledge (Perkins and Salomon 1989).

Reviews of examinations are important not only in improving their reliability and validity. Whether valid or not, examinations are perceived by students as expressing institutional objectives and have a major impact on student learning (Cilliers et al. 2010). Changing an examination has been shown to change teaching and learning (Larsen et al. 2008). An interim assessment has been shown to stimulate students to increase their formal examination scores (Olde Bekkink et al. 2012). Rotem et al. (1982) have proposed to evaluate the curriculum by analyzing examinations to identify disproportionately emphasized content areas and determine the quality and appropriateness of the examination items.

3.3 Attitudes and Values in Curriculum Evaluations

Curriculum evaluation is usually an unpleasant and threatening experience for course coordinators. Attempts to negotiate an educational program may generate entrenchment in opposing positions and even a hostile response. Still, evaluation is necessary, and its results must be communicated to audiences, such as students, faculty, administrators, practicing physicians, funding agencies, the lay public, and the media. Each of these audiences holds distinct values.

3.3.1 Values of Evaluators

Evaluators strive for recognition and gratification. They attempt to meet, up to a point, the expectations of their audience. However, their evaluation is value-laden, as they choose which data to collect, which to ignore, and how to interpret data. Evaluators value the improvement of educational programs. Some view evaluation as an exercise in communication with multiple audiences. Some value the mere challenge of dealing with a difficult and frustrating task. Some evaluators believe in standing on the side and offering objective advice to the program functionaries while others view themselves as part of the system they observe (Maxwell 1984; Sloan and Watson 2001). The differences between these views reflect at least partly the disagreement among evaluators regarding the unique features of their enterprise.

The main uncertainty in the communication between faculty and their evaluators is how to adapt to the notions of the audience. A disparity between the cognitive level of the evaluator and her/his audience may result in a mismatch of purposes and failed expectations. A faculty member, who thinks in terms of dualism would expect evaluations in terms of "good - carry-on" or "bad – delete" and may be exasperated by evaluations of the specific aspects of the program. Conversely, faculty at higher levels of the cognitive hierarchy may be bored with evaluations presented at lower cognitive levels. Consider a high cognitive level teacher who has repeatedly accomplished his educational objectives. He may be bored with an evaluator who limits himself to the flattering end-product evaluation of the course. Conversely, a low cognitive level successful teacher may feel threatened by an evaluator who addresses briefly the satisfactory product and attempts to improve the course by improving its cost-effectiveness.

3.3.2 Faculty Values

An important facet of the institutional tradition is the degree to which faculty value the teaching component of their mission. In European societies, faculty tenure, recognition, and gratification are conditional to research. Teaching is perceived as necessary for the institution's prestige, but not its main goal. The ideal teaching program is viewed as least interfering with research and patient care. In such schools, faculty respond differently to arguments offered by "insiders" and "outsiders." Insiders are clinicians who have credibility. The ideas of outsiders require careful justification. Professional evaluators are seldom physicians and, therefore, outsiders attempting to distract faculty from their research programs. On the other hand, in societies like Canada, medical education is more equalitarian. It is open to influence by nonphysicians and evaluators. Most "novel" medical schools value the teaching component to a greater extent. They embrace educational professionals as "insiders" with hard funding and faculty status, whose work has academic legitimacy.

3.3.3 Values of Medical Students

On the surface, students would gain the most from the curriculum evaluation. Yet, their values vary according to their circumstances and development. According to Perry, the main development in student values occurs when "the student perceives anew the nature of knowledge and Authority's relation to it. He has discarded obedience in favor of his agency as a maker of meaning. He dares to select, to judge, to build. As he studies, his intent is not simply to conciliate Authority ... but to learn on his initiative" (Perry 1968).

A mismatch between teaching and student values may result in intense anxiety and even hostility when students who want precise directions fail to receive them, and in boredom and frustration if students who aspire to permissiveness are not granted freedom to learn. Here again, students at different developmental levels may value teaching differently. For example, some students who hear a lecture on theories of light propagation may expect to be taught which theory is correct and may respond with a cynical nihilism ("nobody knows anything") when they realize that the answer (photons or waves) depends on the context. Other students may perceive the lecturer as poorly qualified since he does not know how light propagates. Still, other students would understand that presently available evidence is compatible with either theory. Each of these students will rate differently the lecturer's performance. One may speculate that students least satisfied with a teaching program benefit most in cognitive development.

3.4 Summing Up

Evidence of an effective program should be sought in student and teacher performance, and a balanced approach to program evaluation should include process and outcome measures. Curriculum design, implementation, and evaluation may be viewed as an integrated unit. The educational needs, present and anticipated, lead to the formulation of educational objectives, then to the design of teaching content, methods of instruction, and program implementation; appropriate examinations may detect deficiencies in its outcome and revise the educational needs. I feel that the evaluation of this closed loop may be improved by considering the following changes.

3.4.1 Improvement of Instruments for Curriculum Evaluation

Summative paper and pencil examinations and student ratings will probably continue to be the mainstay of curriculum evaluation. Therefore, a major effort should be invested in improving their reliability, validity, and usefulness. For example, medical schools may wish to consider first, soliciting students' opinions on how the learning environment and course design can be improved, rather than using questionnaires designed to assess students' global satisfaction with teaching. Second, reviewing the content of tests to ensure their consistency with educational objectives. Test analysis is rarely used to detect gaps in learners' knowledge and to define educational needs. The congruity between faculty intentions, the implemented curriculum, and test structure is seldom explored. I believe that questions such as: "Is the content of the examination consistent with what we believe is the most important?" or "Do the results of the examinations identify serious gaps in student knowledge?" should be more frequently asked.

Third, adding practice ("oral") examinations of student clinical competence as an evaluation measure. Although of limited reliability, oral examinations are a powerful message for students that history taking and information management, physical diagnosis skills, and the ability to discuss the various aspects of a clinical case are among the educational objectives of their education. Finally, gaining an insight into the learning environment ("implicit curriculum," "ethos") by asking questions such as: "Is what is happening with students in the clinical wards indeed what we intended?"

The implicit curriculum teaches important lessons and shapes students' attitudes by using occasional expressions ("Family physicians do not even know how to write a referral note"), or questions perceived to be better avoided ("Why are things done here differently than in the other medical service?"). In addition, an effort should be made to identify the "null curriculum", which consists of the options students are not afforded and the concepts and skills not included in teaching. For example, evaluators should ask why medical schools require fluency in sciences but not in medical economics, psychology, and research methods in the behavioral sciences.

3.4.2 Comprehensive Summative Examination and Counseling of Medical Students

I suggest that medical school summative examinations at the end of the undergraduate program be expanded to include the global ratings of students' performance during the clerkship rotations and testing for students' non-academic attributes that some medical schools use for selecting applicants. The results of these tests and preceptors' evaluations will serve as a starting point for feedback and counseling. Feedback providers would emphasize the limitations of the non-academic attribute tests and discuss students' future careers in an atmosphere of mutual respect and without value judgment.

References

Al-Eyd G, Achike F, Agarwal M, Atamna H, Atapattu DN, Castro L, Estrada J, Ettarh R, Hassan S, Lakhan SE, Nausheen F. Curriculum mapping as a tool to facilitate curriculum development: a new School of Medicine experience. BMC Med Educ. 2018;18(1):1–8.
Berk RA. Top five flashpoints in the assessment of teaching effectiveness. Med Teach. 2013;35(1):15–26.
Boerboom TB, Mainhard T, Dolmans DH, Scherpbier AJ, Van Beukelen P, Jaarsma AD. Evaluating clinical teachers with the Maastricht clinical teaching questionnaire: how much 'teacher' is in student ratings? Med Teach. 2012;34:320–6.
Chan CYW, Sum MY, Tan GMY, Tor PC, Sim K. Adoption and correlates of the Dundee ready educational environment measure (DREEM) in the evaluation of undergraduate learning environments—a systematic review. Med Teach. 2018;40:1240–7.
Cilliers FJ, Schuwirth LW, Adendorff HJ, Herman N, Van der Vleuten CP. The mechanism of impact of summative assessment on medical students' learning. Adv Health Sci Educ. 2010;15:695–715.
Clack GB. Medical graduates evaluate the effectiveness of their education. Med Educ. 1994;28(5):418–31.
Clayson DE. Student evaluations of teaching: are they related to what students learn? A meta-analysis and review of the literature. J Mark Educ. 2009;31(1):16–30.
Donnon T, Delver H, Beran T. Student and teaching characteristics related to ratings of instruction in medical sciences graduate programs. Med Teach. 2010;32:327–32.
Dyrbye LN, Thomas MR, Harper W, Massie FS, Power DV, Eacker A, Szydlo DW, Novotny PJ, Sloan JA, Shanafelt TD. The learning environment and medical student burnout: a multicenter study. Med Educ. 2009;43:274–82.
Epstein RM, Hundert EM. Defining and assessing professional competence. JAMA. 2002;287(2):226–35.

Goldfarb S, Morrison G. Continuous curricular feedback: a formative evaluation approach to curricular improvement. Acad Med. 2014;89:264–9.

Harden RM. AMEE guide no. 21: curriculum mapping: a tool for transparent and authentic teaching and learning. Med Teach. 2001;23:123–37.

Hecker KG, Donahue M, Kaba A, Veale P, Coderre S, McLaughlin K. Summative assessment of Interprofessional "collaborative practice" skills in graduating medical students: a validity argument. Acad Med. 2020;95:1763–9.

Helou MA, Keiser V, Feldman M, Santen S, Cyrus JW, Ryan MS. Student Well-being and the learning environment. Clin Teach. 2019;16:362–6.

Hornstein HA. Student evaluations of teaching are inadequate assessment tool for evaluating faculty performance. Cogent Education. 2017;4(1):1304016.

Jones A, McArdle PJ, O'Neill PA. Perceptions of how well graduates are prepared for the role of pre-registration house officer: a comparison of outcomes from a traditional and an integrated PBL curriculum. Med Educ. 2002;36(1):16–25.

Knowles M. The adult learner: a neglected species. Houston, Texas: Gulf Publishing; 1990.

Korsh BM, Negrete VF. Doctor-patient communication. Scient Amer. 1972;227:66–74.

Kulik JA. Student ratings: Validity, utility, and controversy. New Direct Instit Res. 2001;2001:9–25.

Larsen DP, Butler AC, Roediger HL III. Test-enhanced learning in medical education. Med Educ. 2008;42(10):959–66.

Maxwell GS. A rating scale for assessing the quality of responsive/illuminative evaluations. Educ Eval Policy Anal. 1984;6(2):131–8.

Morrow G, Johnson N, Burford B, Rothwell C, Spencer J, Peile E, Davies C, Allen M, Baldauf B, Morrison J, Illing J. Preparedness for practice: the perceptions of medical graduates and clinical teams. Med Teach. 2012;34(2):123–35.

Norcini JJ, Kimball HR, Lipner RS. Certification and specialization: do they matter in the outcome of acute myocardial infarction? Acad Med. 2000;75:1193–8.

Olde Bekkink M, Donders R, van Muijen GN, Ruiter DJ. Challenging medical students with an interim assessment: a positive effect on formal examination score in a randomized controlled study. Adv Health Sci Educ. 2012;17:27–37.

Perkins DN, Salomon G. Are cognitive skills context-bound? Educ Res. 1989;18:16–25.

Perry WG. Forms of intellectual and ethical development in the college years. New York: Holt, Reinhart & Winston; 1968.

Peters WG, van Coppenolle L, Scherpbier AJ. Combined student ratings and self-assessments provide useful feedback for clinical teachers. Adv Health Sci Educ Theory Pract. 2010;15:315–28.

Plaza CM, Draugalis JR, Slack MK, Skrepnek GH, Sauer KA. Curriculum mapping in program assessment and evaluation. Am J Pharm Educ. 2007;71:1–8.

Pololi LH, Evans AT, Nickell L, Reboli AC, Coplit LD, Stuber ML, Vasiliou V, Civian JT, Brennan RT. Assessing the learning environment for medical students: an evaluation of a novel survey instrument in four medical schools. Acad Psychiatry. 2017;41:354–9.

Price EG, Windish DM, Magaziner J, Cooper LA. Assessing the validity of standardized patient ratings of medical students' communication behavior using the Roter interaction analysis system. Patient Educ Couns. 2008;70(1):3–9.

Prince KJ, Van Eijs PW, Boshuizen HP, Van Der Vleuten CP, Scherpbier AJ. General competencies of problem-based learning (PBL) and non-PBL graduates. Med Educ. 2005;39(4):394–401.

Richardson IM. Consumer view on the medical curriculum: a retrospective study of Aberdeen graduates. Med Ed. 1983;17:8–10.

Rotem A, Barrand J, Azman A. Analysis of examinations in curriculum review. Med Educ. 1982;16:3–6.

Rotem A, Ewan CE, Bandaranayake RC. Review of the curriculum using a pathway analysis of learning difficulties. Med Teacher. 1983;5:94–5.

Schiekirka S, Raupach T. A systematic review of factors influencing student ratings in undergraduate medical education course evaluations. BMC Med Educ. 2015;15(1):1–9.

Sharma M, Murphy R, Doody GA. Do we need a core curriculum for medical students? A scoping review. BMJ Open. 2019;9(8):e027369.

Silber JH, Kennedy SK, Even-Shoshan O. Anesthesiologist board certification and patient outcomes. Anesthesiology. 2002;96:1044–52.

Sloan G, Watson H. Illuminative evaluation: evaluating clinical supervision on its performance rather than the applause. J Adv Nurs. 2001;35(5):664–73.

Stenhouse L. An introduction to curriculum research and development. London: Heinemann; 1971.

Svanum S, Aigner C. The influences of course effort, mastery and performance goals, grade expectancies, and earned course grades on student ratings of course satisfaction. Br J Educ Psychol. 2011;81:667–79.

Tackett S, Wright S, Lubin R, Li J, Pan H. International study of medical school learning environments and their relationship with student Well-being and empathy. Med Educ. 2017;51:280–9.

Tallentire VR, Smith SE, Skinner J, Cameron HS. The preparedness of UK graduates in acute care: a systematic literature review. Postgrad Med J. 2012;88:365–71.

Terry R, Hing W, Orr R, Milne N. Do coursework summative assessments predict clinical performance? A systematic review. BMC Med Educ. 2017;17:40.

Wass V, Van der Vleuten C, Shatzer J, Jones R. Assessment of clinical competence. Lancet. 2001;357(9260):945–9.

Wayne SJ, Fortner SA, Kitzes JA, Timm C, Kalishman S. Cause or effect? The relationship between student perception of the medical school learning environment and academic performance on USMLE step 1. Med Teach. 2013;35:376–80.

Wilkinson TJ, Fontaine S. Patients' global ratings of student competence. Unreliable contamination or gold standard? Med Educ. 2002;36(12):1117–21.

Wright B, McKendree J, Morgan L, Allgar VL, Brown A. Examiner and simulated patient ratings of empathy in medical student final year clinical examination: are they useful? BMC Med Educ. 2014;14(1):1–8.

Chapter 4
Quality Control of Education

Abstract Most schools have established medical education units (MEUs) to provide educational support to their faculty. Furthermore, to ensure the quality of undergraduate medical programs, most countries conduct periodic external reviews of medical schools to ascertain their compliance with accreditation standards. The aims of this section are, first, to describe the function of MEUs; second to propose that they become independent departments dedicated to monitoring the preparation for accreditation through continuous self-evaluation of teaching; and third, to suggest that this monitoring consider a four-tiered classification of accreditation standards according to the strength of evidence for their importance.

4.1 Medical Education Units

To provide educational support to their faculty, medical schools have established education units (MEUs), and, to assure the quality of the undergraduate programs of their medical schools, most countries conduct periodic external reviews of medical schools to ascertain their compliance with accreditation standards. Thus, the Liaison Committee on Medical Education (LCME) provides accreditation for schools of medicine in the United States and Canada (Liaison Committee on Medical Education 2010); The General Medical Council provides accreditation for schools of medicine in the UK (Tomorrow's Doctors 2009); and the World Federation for Medical Education (WFME) is an international organization dedicated to enhancing the quality of medical education worldwide (World Federation for Medical Education 2012).

Medical education units are expected to contribute to the institution's vision and mission, recommend reforms, and enhance scholarly activity. MEUs can help

---

A previous version of parts of this chapter was published in Benbassat J, Baumal R, Cohen R. Quality Assurance of Undergraduate Medical Education in Israel by Continuous Monitoring and Prioritization of the Accreditation Standards. Rambam Maimonides Medical Journal. 2022 Jul;13(3). With permission from the editor.

teachers consider alternative solutions to specific problems by encouraging reflective rather than intuitive decisions and informing faculty about novel teaching and student assessment methods. However, MEUs have existed only since the 1950s and their functions vary according to the interests of their members, funding, faculty expectations, and local traditions. In 2008, North American MEUs employed on average five professional and faculty staff supported by university funds, research and training grants, and contracts with other institutions (Gruppen 2008).

MEUs vary in levels of activity. For example, they may consist of the presence of a MEU member in faculty committees and providing advice when needed. Alternatively, she/he may distribute a paper summarizing the currently available information on the topic to be discussed and the pros and cons of alternative options. Similarly, the MEU's contribution to student assessment may be limited to using an optical scanner and communicating the test results to examiners. Alternatively, it may provide feedback on the examinee's performance on individual test items, identify knowledge gaps, and improve teaching by filling them. It may also include advice on the content, number of questions, and coverage of the material being examined, or workshops on writing test items.

There are several models of MEUs. The first one provides a single service, such as student assessment. The second is that in the innovative medical schools, such as MacMaster. Their founders dominated the planning and implementation of the undergraduate program. A third model of MEUs assigns to the various departments a permanent advisor who acquires a deeper insight into the teaching needs of each of them. A fourth model assumes the added responsibility for courses on the Behavioral Sciences in Medicine and the doctor-patient relationship, thereby portraying the unit as part of the teaching faculty and not merely an advisory body. Finally, although initially intended to support their home institutions, the units in the Universities of New South Wells in Sydney and of Illinois in Chicago eventually became grant-funded and independent, and their main function evolved into research and provision of consulting services outside their institutions.

4.2 External Reviews for Accreditation of Medical Schools

The external reviews for accreditation require medical schools to perform a self-evaluation of their programs. This self-evaluation helps the accreditation committee prepare for the site visit. This visit includes a review of documentation, inspections, and meetings with faculty and students. After the visit, the committee provides the deans with its initial findings, and several months later, with final recommendations. Although its main purpose is to improve the educational processes in medical schools, accreditation is subject to several types of uncertainties and criticism.

First, accreditation visits in North America occur at 4–10-year intervals and do not identify problems promptly (Barzansky et al. 2015). Second, the accreditation standards are not equally important. Experts were reported to agree that only 14 of the 150 standards of the World Federation of Medical Education (WFME) were essential and to disagree about the importance of the remaining standards (Van Zanten et al. 2012). The UK General Medical Council (GMC) and WFME distinguish between standards that *must* and *should* be met. The Liaison Committee of Medical Education (LCME) discerns between standards that, if not complied with, place a teaching program at *immediate* and *lesser* risks. Nevertheless, I know of no agreed-upon taxonomy of standards, and consequently, the differences in their importance do not figure meaningfully in the accreditation process. Third, a 2021 review of the literature indicated that even though faculty and students recognized the merits of accreditation (e.g., switching to active learning), they also recognized its unintended negative consequences (e.g., faculty distraction from teaching in favor of accreditation bureaucracy) (Choa et al. 2021).

In response to this criticism, Barzansky et al. (2015) proposed to "… engage in ongoing … continuous quality improvement processes … [and] ensure effective monitoring of the medical education program's compliance with accreditation standards." This suggestion has been adopted also by the accreditation authorities in the West. Indeed, *continuous* monitoring of the teaching programs has been shown to improve the learning environment, career advising, teaching the physical examination, clerkship feedback, and communication with faculty and other stakeholders (Hedrick et al. 2019).

The literature review by Choa et al. (2021) indicated that faculty and students thought that a dedicated unit overseeing the quality assurance and preparation for accreditation would improve the management of the curriculum, and I suggest assigning this monitoring to MEUs. Continuous monitoring of the implementation of the teaching program would ensure the outcomes of the evaluations by accreditation committees. However, criticism will likely generate confrontations, even when faculty understand the importance of meeting these standards. I have heard faculty repeatedly blame MEU members for being oblivious to the realities of clinical practice, and MEU members claim that clinicians are ignorant of the basic teaching principles. Defining one of the functions of MEUs as continuous monitoring of the curriculum and the degree of its accord with accreditation standards may reduce this polarization, since both MEU and faculty members would be united in a common purpose, to wit, meeting accreditation standards.

4.3 Prioritization of Accreditation Standards

Barzansky et al. (2015) raised the question of whether all accreditation standards should guide monitoring of the curriculum, or only selected accreditation standards and, if the latter, how they must be chosen. To answer this question, I propose prioritizing the accreditation standards by the strength of evidence for their importance.

A straightforward validation of the accreditation standards would demonstrate their association *with student well-being* and *patient health outcomes*. However, until 2000, most teaching interventions were assessed only by their face validity and association with student learning and satisfaction, and only 0.7% of the studies used patient outcomes as an indicator of teaching effectiveness (Prystowsky and Bordage 2001). It was only in the last two decades that research has used patient health outcomes for validation of teaching programs, and the advent of electronic medical records holds the potential of using big data to improve care by linking clinical outcomes to educational programs. In 2022, my colleagues and I proposed a four-tier prioritization of the LCME accreditation standards according to their validation level (Table 4.1).

4.3.1 Level 1: The Most Important Accreditation Standards

The "most important" standards are those associated with student well-being and, in practicing doctors, with improved patient health outcomes. These include the LCME requirements about *Learning environment* (Standards 3, 3.5); *teaching communication skills* (Standard 7.8); *use of simulations in teaching* (Standard 7.3); *Students' assessment* (Standard 9); *and Students' counseling* (Standard 11) (Tables 4.1 and 4.2).

Table 4.1 Proposed classification of the standards for medical school accreditation by strength of validation. Adapted with permission from Benbassat et al. 2022

Accreditation standard (*LCME Item #*) [a]	Justification for inclusion into the level of importance
Level 1: Most important standards—Standards associated with students' Well-being or patients' health outcomes	
"A medical school ... program occurs in professional, respectful, and intellectually stimulating ... environment" (3) where "... all individuals are treated with respect" (3.5)	The learning environment is the main source of students' distress (Tackett et al. 2017). Its positive perception is associated with reduced student burnout (Dyrbye et al. 2009), better learning (Wayne et al. 2013), quality of life, resilience, preparedness for practice, and well-being (Chan et al. 2018; Helou et al. 2019)
"The curriculum includes instruction in communication skills" (7.8)	Teaching communication skills improves patients' satisfaction with care, adherence to recommendations, and health outcomes in hypertensive patients (Zolnierek and DiMatteo 2009; Tavakoly Sany et al. 2018)
"The curriculum includes ... simulated exercises" (7.3)	The use of skill simulation laboratories is superior to traditional training and leads to small-moderate patient benefits (Mundell et al. 2013; Cook et al. 2013; Zendejas et al. 2013)
"A medical program includes a comprehensive, fair, and uniform system of ... medical student assessment" (9)	Performance on examinations in medical school predicts performance in the internship and clinical practice (Terry et al. 2017; Hecker et al. 2020). Patients treated by cardiologists (Norcini et al. 2000) and anesthesiologists (Silber et al. 2002) who had passed the board examinations have better health outcomes than patients treated by non-certified care providers

(continued)

4.3 Prioritization of Accreditation Standards

Table 4.1 (continued)

Accreditation standard (*LCME Item #*) [a]	Justification for inclusion into the level of importance
A medical school provides "… effective academic support and career advising to all medical students" (11, 12.3)	Improving the learning environment, and teaching students how to use psychological and emotional support resources reduce student depression and anxiety rates (Slavin 2019)
Level 2: Important standards—Standards associated with student learning and/or performance	
A medical school "…Engages in continuous quality improvement processes that … ensure … program's compliance with accreditation standards" (1.1). "… has in place a body … that oversees the medical education program" (8.1)	Continuous monitoring of the teaching programs for compliance with accreditation standards improves the learning environment, career advising, teaching the physical examination, clerkship feedback, and communication with faculty and other stakeholders (Hedrick et al. 2019)
The medical school "… ensures that each medical student is assessed and provided with formal formative feedback" (9.7)	Formative examinations improve clinical performance (Ivers et al. 2012), learning (Saint et al. 2015), and development of professional behavior (Lerchenfeldt et al. 2019)
A medical school "… provides opportunities for professional development to each faculty member" (4.5)	Faculty development programs affect self-reported faculty enhanced confidence and comfort with their teaching, higher student ratings, and improved academic ability in terms of publications and conference presentations (Alexandraki et al. 2021)
A medical school "… has formal processes… to collect and consider medical student evaluations of their courses, clerkships, and teachers" (8.5)	The use of student feedback to course directors improves teaching programs (Kulik 2001; Boerboom et al. 2012; Goldfarb & Morrison 2014; Peters et al. 2010)
The medical curriculum "includes clinical experiences in both outpatient and inpatient settings" (6.4)	Students rate clerkships in a single general practice setting higher than traditional clerkships for teaching, feedback, role-modeling, and patient-centered experiences (Walters et al. 2012)

[a]*LCME* Liaison Committee on Medical Education

Table 4.2 (continued): Proposed classification of the standards for medical school accreditation by strength of validation

Accreditation standard (*LCME Item #*) [a]	Justification for inclusion into the level of importance
Level 3: Possibly important standards—Standards with face validity, or with conflicting evidence for association with student learning	
A medical school "… defines its program objectives in outcome-based terms" (6.1)	Compelling face validity. Conflicting evidence for association with student learning (Slaughenhoupt et al. 2011; Wyte et al. 1995; McLaughlin et al. 2005)
A medical school "…has a sufficient number of faculty in leadership roles and of administrative staff … necessary to achieve the goals of the education program" (2)	Compelling face validity

(continued)

Table 4.2 (continued)

Accreditation standard (*LCME Item #*) [a]	Justification for inclusion into the level of importance
Level 4: Least important—Standards with possible unintended consequences	
A medical school "… selects applicants for admission who possess the intelligence, integrity, and personal and emotional characteristics necessary for them to become competent physicians" (10.4)	Conflicting evidence that selection for non-cognitive attributes predicts students' performance. Such selection may reduce the self-esteem of rejected applicants' and may not justify its cost (Schreurs et al. 2020; Patterson et al. 2016; Norman 2004)
Use of student ratings of *individual* teachers to inform academic promotions (4.4)	Conflicting evidence that student ratings of individual teachers are associated with teaching effectiveness (Donnon et al. 2010; Svanum & Aigner 2011). The use of student ratings of individual teachers to inform academic promotions may contribute to student-faculty alienation

[a]*LCME* Liaison Committee on Medical Education

4.3.2 Level 2: Important Standards

The "important" accreditation standards are those associated with student learning or performance. They include *periodic evaluation and revision of the teaching program* (Standards 8, 8.4); *formative examinations* (9.7); and *faculty professional development* (4.5). This category includes Standard 8.5 which requires *student evaluations of their courses*. As detailed in Chap. 3, the validity of student ratings of individual teachers is uncertain. While they have been shown to improve teaching courses (Goldfarb & Morrison 2014), the ratings of individual instructors to inform academic promotions may have undesirable consequences as detailed below. This category also includes Standard 6.4 which requires *clinical experience in both outpatient and inpatient settings*. Some medical schools have introduced "integrated clerkships" programs to be discussed in Chap. 5.

4.3.3 Level 3: Possibly Important Standards

This level consists of standards with face validity or conflicting evidence for validity. It includes Standard 2 which requires faculty in leadership roles and senior administrative staff with the skills, time, and administrative support necessary to achieve the goals of the medical education program. This standard has compelling face validity as even a program with a superb curriculum would not maintain itself without resources and governance. Standard 6.1 requires a *definition of learning objectives*. This requirement has a similarly compelling face validity because intended outcomes underpin all teaching, learning, and assessment activities. However, their association with student outcomes is uncertain.

4.3.4 Level 4: Least Important Standards

This level includes controversial standards that may lead to unintended negative consequences. Standard 10.4 calls for an admissions policy that selects applicants with the personal and emotional qualities necessary for the profession of medicine. The uncertain validity of this selection is discussed in Chap. 7. It has been suggested that the stated pursuit of personal qualities can affect the self-esteem of rejected applicants, particularly if they are left wondering if there is something wrong with their character (Norman 2004).

Standard 4.4 requires *students' ratings of individual teachers*. Such ratings may provide useful feedback and improve teaching effectiveness (Kulik 2001). However, students' ratings may be biased by workload, motivation, and anticipated success on examinations. Therefore, while student ratings of courses and student feedback to individual teachers should be considered an important standard, using student ratings to inform decisions for academic promotions may be humiliating, contribute to student-faculty alienation, and should be among the least important standards.

4.4 Summing Up

The described four-level classification of the accreditation standards is consistent with the recommendation that the choice of learning objectives and teaching content should derive from patients' health outcomes, rather than from tradition and gut feelings ("evidence-guided education") (Glick 2005). The proposed prioritization is also consistent with some previously identified important accreditation standards (van Zanten et al. 2012; Hunt et al. 2016), such as teaching clinical skills and assessing students' learning.

Non-compliance with "most important" and "important" standards would require urgent attention, and their correction should gain precedence over non-compliance with the remaining standards. For example, earlier I referred to my belief that the perceived quality of the clinical learning environment is the most important accreditation standard. MEUs can obtain an insight into this environment through student debriefing, focus groups, and student surveys aimed at obtaining information on students' reflections on what they find difficult, their experiences, critical incidents, learner-faculty relationship, and the degree to which faculty support students in distress, at all times and especially during the clinical rotations. Negative student perceptions of their learning environment would justify immediate remediation.

Monitoring the curriculum is of no value without a mechanism to ensure that the elicited information is acted upon. Hence the need for a policy aimed at creating MEUs with appropriately trained staff and budget, the foremost function of which would be the continuous evaluation of the implementation of the teaching program, and helping faculty correct detected flaws. MEUs would be part of the governance of the medical school and have the authority to implement interventions (Benbassat et al. 2022). Yet, it is uncertain from whom MEUs would draw their authority. The term "self-evaluation" implies that they would have the backing and support of the Dean. However, in Israel, Deans are elected for short terms. Most of them have limited knowledge of how to assess teaching programs. To be effective, MEUs cannot risk being vetoed by the Dean, particularly when she or he cancels a specific effort to improve the educational process. Therefore, policies need to be developed to establish a meaningful role of the MEUs in medical schools. For example, MEUs may draw authority from university institutions that would have to rule in the hopefully exceptional cases of disagreement between the MEU and the Dean.

References

Alexandraki I, Rosasco RE, Mooradian AD. An evaluation of faculty development programs for clinician–educators: a scoping review. Acad Med. 2021;91:599–606.

Barzansky B, Hunt D, Moineau G, Ahn D, Lai CW, Humphrey H, Peterson L. Continuous quality improvement in an accreditation system for undergraduate medical education: benefits and challenges. Med Teach. 2015;37:1032–8.

Benbassat J, Baumal R, Cohen R. Quality Assurance of Undergraduate Medical Education in Israel by Continuous Monitoring and Prioritization of the Accreditation Standards. Rambam Maimonides Med J. 2022;13(3):e0023.

Boerboom TB, Mainhard T, Dolmans DH, Scherpbier AJ, Van Beukelen P, Jaarsma AD. Evaluating clinical teachers with the Maastricht clinical teaching questionnaire: how much 'teacher' is in student ratings? Med Teach. 2012;34:320–6.

Chan CYW, Sum MY, Tan GMY, Tor PC, Sim K. Adoption and correlates of the Dundee Ready Educational Environment Measure (DREEM) in the evaluation of undergraduate learning environments - a systematic review. Med Teach. 2018;40:1240–1247.

Choa G, Arfeen Z, Chan SC, Rashid MA. Understanding impacts of accreditation on medical teachers and students: a systematic review and meta-ethnography. Med Teach. 2021;44:1–8.

Cook DA, Hamstra SJ, Brydges R, Zendejas B, Szostek JH, Wang AT, Erwin PJ, Hatala R. Comparative effectiveness of instructional design features in simulation-based education: systematic review and meta-analysis. Med Teach. 2013;35:e867–98.

Donnon T, Delver H, Beran T. Student and teaching characteristics related to ratings of instruction in medical sciences graduate programs. Medical Teacher. 2010;32:327–332.

Dyrbye LN, Thomas MR, Harper W, Massie FS, Power DV, Eacker A, Szydlo DW, Novotny PJ, Sloan JA, Shanafelt TD. The learning environment and medical student burnout: a multicenter study. Medical Education. 2009;43:274–282.

Glick TH. Evidence-guided education: patients' outcome data should influence our teaching priorities. Acad Med. 2005;80(2):147–51.

Goldfarb S, Morrison G. Continuous curricular feedback: a formative evaluation approach to curricular improvement. Academic Medicine. 2014;89:264–269.

Gruppen L. Creating and sustaining centers for medical education research and development. Med Educ. 2008;42:121–2.

Hecker KG, Donahue M, Kaba A, Veale P, Coderre S, McLaughlin K. Summative Assessment of Interprofessional "Collaborative Practice" Skills in Graduating Medical Students: A Validity Argument. Acad Med. 2020;95:1763–1769.

Hedrick JS, Cottrell S, Stark D, Brownfield E, Stoddard HA, Angle SM, Buckley LA, Clinch CR, Esposito K, Krane NK, Park V, Teal CR, Ferrari ND. A review of continuous quality improvement processes at ten medical schools. Med Sci Educ. 2019;29:285–90.

References

Helou MA, Keiser V, Feldman M, Santen S, Cyrus JW, Ryan MS. Student well-being and the learning environment. Clin Teach. 2019;16:362–366.

Hunt D, Migdal M, Waechter DM, Barzansky B, Sabalis RF. The variables that lead to severe action decisions by the liaison committee on medical education. Acad Med. 2016;91(1):87–93.

Ivers N, Jamtvedt G, Flottorp S, Young JM, Odgaard-Jensen J, French SD, O'Brien MA, Johansen M, Grimshaw J, Oxman AD. Audit and feedback: effects on professional practice and healthcare outcomes (Review). Cochrane Database of Systematic Reviews 2012, Issue 6. Art. No.: CD000259.

Kulik JA. Student ratings: Validity, utility, and controversy. New Direct Inst Res. 2001;2001:9–25.

Lerchenfeldt S, Mi M, Eng M. The utilization of peer feedback during collaborative learning in undergraduate medical education: a systematic review. BMC Med Educ. 2019;19:321.

Liaison Committee on Medical Education (LCME) for the USA. Functions and structure of a medical school. 2010. https://medicine.vtc.vt.edu/content/dam/medicine. Accessed Jan 2022.

McLaughlin K, Coderre S, Woloschuk W, Lim T, Muruve D, Mandin H. The influence of objectives, learning experiences and examination blueprint on medical students' examination preparation. BMC Med Educ. 2005;5:1–6.

Mundell WC, Kennedy CC, Szostek JH, Cook DA. Simulation technology for resuscitation training: a systematic review and meta-analysis. Resuscitation. 2013;84:1174–83.

Norcini JJ, Kimball HR, Lipner RS. Certification and specialization: Do they matter in the outcome of acute myocardial infarction? Academic Medicine. 2000;75:1193–1198.

Norman G. The morality of medical school admissions. Advances in Health Sciences Education. 2004;9:79–82.

Patterson F, Knight A, Dowell J, Nicholson S, Cousans F, Cleland J. How effective are selection methods in medical education? A systematic review. Medical Education. 2016;50:36–60.

Peters WG, van Coppenolle L, Scherpbier AJ. Combined student ratings and self-assessments provide useful feedback for clinical teachers. Adv Health Sci Educ Theory Pract. 2010;15:315–28.

Prystowsky JB, Bordage G. An outcome research perspective on medical education: the predominance of trainee assessment and satisfaction. Med Educ. 2001;35:331–6.

Saint DA, Horton D, Yool A, Elliott A. A progressive assessment strategy improves student learning and perceived course quality in undergraduate physiology. Adv Physiol Educ. 2015;39:218–22.

Schreurs S, Cleutjens KBJM, Cleland J, Oude Egbrink MGA. Outcomes-based selection into medical school: predicting excellence in multiple competencies during the clinical years. Acad Med. 2020;95:1411–20.

Silber JH, Kennedy SK, Even-Shoshan O. Anesthesiologist board certification and patient outcomes. Anesthesiology. 2002;96:1044–1052.

Slaughenhoupt BL, Lester RA, Rowe JM, Wollack JA. Design, implementation, and evaluation of a new core learning objectives curriculum for a urology clerkship. J Urol. 2011;186:1417–21.

Slavin S. Reflections on a Decade Leading a Medical Student Well-Being Initiative. Acad Med. 2019;94:771–4.

Tackett S, Wright S, Lubin R, Li J, Pan H. International study of medical school learning environments and their relationship with student well-being and empathy. Medical Education. 2017;51:280–289.

Tavakoly Sany SB, Peyman N, Behzhad F, Esmaeily H, Taghipoor A, Ferns G. Health providers' communication skills training affects hypertension outcomes. Med Teach. 2018;40(2):154–63.

Terry R, Hing W, Orr R, Milne N. Do coursework summative assessments predict clinical performance? A systematic review. BMC Med Educ. 2017;17:40.

Tomorrow's Doctors. Outcomes and standards for undergraduate medical education. 2009. http://www.gmc-uk.org/Tomorrows Doctors_48905759.pdf. April 2021.

Van Zanten M, Boulet JR, Greaves I. The importance of medical education accreditation standards. Med Teach. 2012;34:136–45.

Walters L, Greenhill J, Richards J, Ward H, Campbell N, Ash J, Schuwirth LW. Outcomes of longitudinal integrated clinical placements for students, clinicians, and society. Med Educ. 2012;46(11):1028–41.

Wayne SJ, Fortner SA, Kitzes JA, Timm C, Kalishman S. Cause or effect? The relationship between student perception of the medical school learning environment and academic performance on USMLE Step 1. Medical Teacher. 2013;35:376–380.

World Federation for Medical Education. Basic Medical Education WFME Global Standards for Quality Improvement. 2012. https://www.um.es/documents/1935287/1936044/. Revision of Standards for Basic Medical Education in April 2021.

Wyte C, Pitts F, Cabel JA, Yarnold PR, Bare A, Adams SL. Effect of learning objectives on the performances of students and interns rotating through an emergency department. Acad Med. 1995;70:1145.

Zendejas B, Brydges R, Wang AT, Cook DA. Patient outcomes in simulation-based medical education: a systematic review. Journal of General Internal Medicine 2013;28:1078–1089.

Zolnierek KBH, DiMatteo MR. Physician communication and patient adherence to treatment: a meta-analysis. Med Care. 2009;47:826–34.

Chapter 5
Curriculum Innovations and Alternative Models of Medical Education

Abstract Since the 1950s, newly established medical schools have adopted novel curricular designs such as the organ-system model (Case Western) and the Flexible (elective) model (Duke University School of Medicine). The traditional knowledge-oriented programs were replaced with mission-oriented curricula emphasizing skill acquisition. Although committed to problem-solving rather than knowledge, most innovative curricula have invested efforts to improve learning efficiency, and rigid teaching programs were replaced with programs matched to individual students by allowing each of them to learn at his/her pace.

This section describes four curricular innovations: the problem-based, self-directed learning model, the early exposure of students to patients, the integrated longitudinal clerkship model in primary care clinics, and the shift to accepting uncertainty in clinical practice.

5.1 Theoretical Models of Disease and Medical Training

Doctors have always relied on theoretical models to understand diseases. If these models met clinical needs and were consistent with current experience, they were used to interpret clinical reality and guide research. A change in the model occurs only when it can no longer accommodate new data (Kuhn 1970). For example, the biomedical model has dominated medical teaching and practice since the nineteenth century. This model views diseases as structural or biochemical disorders and assumes that patient care should be derived from the etiology and pathophysiology of the disease. However, by the end of the twentieth century, physicians realized that pathophysiologic logic does not always lead to expected outcomes. They became aware of the association between life events and morbidity on one side and between socioeconomic status and mortality on the other. This realization led to the adoption of evidence-based medicine (EBM) (Guyatt et al. 1992) and bio-psycho-social medicine (Engel 1977, 1992) as current models of clinical practice.

Another example relates to the organization of health care. Until the 1960s, clinical practice was centralized and hierarchical. Departmental heads decided how to care for patients and how to teach medicine. However, the increase in biomedical knowledge and technology led to a proliferation of sub-specialties with a decline in the authority of the departmental head. The goal of medical education moved from knowledge acquisition and its application in patient care to helping students develop critical thinking, lifelong self-directed learning habits, and the ability to retrieve information from data stores (Ludmerer 2004). Clinical reasoning became less deterministic, more probabilistic, less "intuitive" and more anchored to evidence. Attempts to reconstruct the cause and pathogenesis of the disease (What happened?) were replaced with an acknowledgment of the uncertainties in diagnosis, treatment, and prognosis (What will happen?). The view that disease causation may be reduced to biochemical and structural disorders was replaced with the bio-psychosocial model of clinical practice that recognizes emotional, social, and interpersonal causes of disease.

5.2 The Problem-Based, Self-Directed Learning Model

The problem-based learning (PBL) model was introduced at McMaster University in Ontario in the 1960s. It is the most sustained innovation adopted in medical schools across North America and Europe (Campbell 1970). PBL expects learners to assume responsibility for their learning and develop a solution to a defined problem. Students work in collaborative small groups to identify what they need to know to solve the problem, engage in self-directed learning, and apply their new knowledge to the problem. The function of the student's tutor is critical to PBL; therefore, its implementation requires tutor-training programs.

A 2010 review of the literature revealed that 12 of 15 studies that compared PBL with traditional medical students found no significant differences in knowledge acquisition as measured by exam scores. Three of four studies found better diagnostic accuracy and some detected improved clerkship, internship, or residency performance of PBL graduates (Hartling et al. 2010). A 2022 review confirmed that PBL improved student satisfaction and was more effective than traditional (lecture-based) methods at imparting social and communication skills, problem-solving, and self-directed learning. Knowledge retention and academic performance were not worse (and in many studies were better) than traditional methods (Trullàs et al. 2022).

Yet, PBL is not widespread, probably because it requires more human resources and tutor training for its implementation. Furthermore, PBL students achieved lower scores on basic sciences examinations (Albanese and Mitchell 1993), needed more time to find a postgraduate training place (Cohen-Schotanus et al. 2008), and were more likely to agree that they did not know what the faculty expected of them (Lewis et al. 2009).

5.3 Early Student Exposure to Patients

The medical school of the Ben-Gurion University in Israel was founded in the 1970s. Its main innovation was student exposure to patients already in the first half of the six-year undergraduate program (Benor 1987). The broad goals of the early clinical program (ECP) were to explain the relevance of the basic sciences for clinical practice, impart basic clinical skills, facilitate students' professional socialization, and teach the principles of clinical problem-solving and management of uncertainty.

The duration of the ECP is three years. It includes first concepts of the natural history of the disease, such as risk indicators, diagnosis, hospitalization, and rehabilitation, as well as knowledge of the human life cycle, surface anatomy, epidemiology (significance tests), and the structure and function of the health services. Second, skills: patient interviewing, physical examination, and emergency medicine. Third, attitudes: socialization into the medical profession and acceptance of other health professionals as members of the health care team.

Unlike PBL, I know of no studies comparing ECP graduates with those of traditional medical curricula. Students' debriefings (Benbassat 1992, unpublished observations) have indicated that they were mostly satisfied with the program. Yet they felt that patient interviews were repetitive and boring; that some clinical experiences made them feel just "hanging around"; that some PBL instructors ignored issues raised by the students, and focused on those which they, the instructors, had prepared in advance; and that not all of them had mastered elementary medical procedures, such subcutaneous and intramuscular injections. Most students perceived statistics and epidemiology as less relevant for clinical work than the basic sciences, and some could not explain the relevance of test characteristics for clinical practice.

5.4 Longitudinal Integrated Clerkships

Clinical undergraduate education follows the tradition of "bedside" teaching. It exposes medical students to inpatients. Until the 1960s, patients with a variety of illnesses had to be referred to hospitals due to the lack of community consultation services. Since then, however, the development of community consultation services has limited inpatients primarily to those requiring crisis intervention. Consequently, medical students can now graduate without ever seeing patients with a range of non-acute conditions such as hypothyroidism, peptic ulcers, uncomplicated rheumatoid arthritis, influenza, and tonsillitis treated in community clinics. Medical students also do not see chronic patients treated at home, hospice, or chronic care facilities who only come to the hospital for an acute event. Furthermore, the undergraduate clinical curriculum is determined mostly by specialists, who often cannot define the differences in their expectations from medical students and residents. The implicit assumption of restricting medical education to hospitals views clinical problem-solving as a general skill that, once acquired, can be applied in other settings. However, this assumption is at odds with evidence that competence is subject-specific rather than general (Perkins and Salomon 1989).

These limitations of the hospital setting for clinical teaching led some medical schools to replace the traditional block clerkships with 6–12 months longitudinal integrated clerkships (LICs) in community clinics where students are exposed to common diseases and follow patients through their entire experience, including hospitalizations. There are two LIC models: community-based LICs where students work in a single general practice and follow patients referred to consultants and through hospitalizations; and ambulatory care-based LICs in specialty care clinics. Both models emphasize the continuity of care and supervision (Walters et al. 2012).

The student-staff relationship in LICs allows for continuity in education, responsiveness to learning needs, and guidance in clinical reasoning (Snow et al. 2017). Continuity of student-patient relationships fosters empathy more than short-term relationships with inpatients. Replacing block clerkships with longitudinal clerkships enhances students' clinical reasoning by exposing them to a broader range of diseases and giving them insight into the thinking and doubts of their tutors (Dube et al. 2019).

When compared to hospital-based clerkship rotations, LIC *faculty* reported increased satisfaction from teaching; improved mentoring skills; improved familiarity with students that permitted tailoring instruction to individual learning needs; asking more questions that promote critical thinking; and providing students with opportunities to engage in clinical reasoning (Snow et al. 2017). Outcome studies have shown that LIC *students* were more satisfied. Despite early disorientation in organizing their learning, students felt supported by the continuity of student-preceptor relationships (Walters et al. 2012), and the performance of LIC students was equivalent to, and in some cases better than, that of their peers who completed block clerkships (Ogrinc et al. 2002; Norris et al. 2009; Walters et al. 2012; Hirsh et al. 2012).

Comparative studies have also found that LIC *graduates* rated faculty teaching, faculty supervision of clinical skills, feedback, and the clerkship overall higher than students of traditional block clerkships. Students felt supported by the continuity of the student-tutor relationship (Brown et al. 2019). LIC students observed more positive role-modeling behaviors, had more patient-centered experiences, and outperformed their counterparts in clinical skills (Teherani et al. 2013). LIC graduates had higher insight into social determinants of illness, and increased commitment to patients (Hirsh et al. 2012; Teherani et al. 2013). They had better patient-centered communication skills, demonstrated an understanding of the psychosocial contributions to medicine, reported more preparedness in clinical skills (Walters et al. 2012; Caygill et al. 2017), and dealt with ethical dilemmas (Brown et al. 2019) than students in traditional block rotations. The performance of graduates of longitudinal primary care clerkships was equivalent to, and in some cases better than that of their peers who completed block clerkships (Teherani et al. 2013; Walters et al. 2012). Finally, if the student-tutor relationship shapes the student's future relationship with their patients (Donetto 2010), LICs may provide an environment that prepares students for patient-centered care. Future studies may examine whether training in community settings improves students' professionalism, moral judgment, and reflective skills.

5.5 Teaching Clinical Reasoning (See Also Sect. 9.6)

Teaching in the 1950s emphasized adherence to routine and thoroughness. It was assumed that the more history, physical, and other data accumulated, the better the chances of making a correct diagnosis. Students were taught to learn facts, and clinical decisions were based on the intuition of authorities. This reinforced a belief that there is no uncertainty; that every question in medicine has one correct answer; and that errors were committed only by a few incompetent physicians.

Today, however, clinical decisions are expected to be clinically sound, economically affordable, and ethically permissible, and education is expected to impart the concepts necessary for such decisions. Medical schools have responded to these expectations by introducing courses in ethics, epidemiology, evidence-based medicine, the economic dimensions of medical practice, and quality of care. However, I believe that the impact of these classroom courses is limited and what is taught may be easily snuffed out by the contradictory environment of the hospital wards. To be effective role models, clinicians must exhibit visibility of their ways of thinking and doubts and emphasize the relevance of statistics in processing clinical information. Students must realize that their uncertainty is shared by their instructors and be given to understand that their doubts do not reflect their incompetence but are rather the essence of medical practice.

As I stated earlier, teaching in the 1950s advocated that the more data obtained, the better the chances of making a correct diagnosis. Today, however, the attitude to diagnostic tests has changed. We are aware that false-positive test results not only increase healthcare costs but may also confound diagnostic reasoning (Galen and Gambino 1975). Consequently, we are selective in choosing diagnostic tests and in screening for disease. We have moved from deterministic to probabilistic reasoning and *from indiscriminate to selective use of clinical testing.*

Another innovation was teaching the concepts of evidence-based medicine and clinical decision-making. Our mental ability to combine clinical and laboratory data in assessing disease probabilities is limited, and rules, such as Bayesian inference, are not readily acquired through experience. Overcoming these barriers requires both students and clinical faculty to realize that any attempt to avoid the biases of intuitive decision-making has, by definition, to be counter-intuitive, and that many scientific theories that help us better understand the world, run counter to plain sense.

Lastly, in 1980 Hilfiker argued that medical school graduates cannot cope with their errors because nothing in their training prepares them to respond appropriately to the mistakes they will inevitably make. The increasing acceptance of error as inevitable will probably lead to the inclusion into the undergraduate curriculum of open discussions of the most frequent errors and causes of patient dissatisfaction. An approach to clinical training based on an analysis of common errors in clinical judgment may even promote learners' well-being, because "one consistent theme [that] seems to emerge from all ... studies of medical students, physicians in residency training and physicians in practice [is]: the fear of personal inadequacy and failure" (Guerrity et al. 1992).

5.6 Summing Up

The traditional designs of undergraduate medical curricula are teacher-centered; they require students to learn a defined content of knowledge; skills are expected to be acquired informally during practice, and exposure to patients is mostly in the hospital setting. On the other hand, innovative approaches assign students the responsibility for learning; knowledge is acquired by self-directed learning; skills are acquired by formal training first, in simulated settings, and then through supervised practice. It is realized that premature implementation of skills may not only harm patients; it also breeds anxiety and prevents learning. Clinical education has shifted to a continuous follow-up of patients in community settings. Emphasis is placed on the ability to cope with familiar and unfamiliar clinical problems, rather than on the acquisition of knowledge.

Dealing with unfamiliar situations requires an emphasis on several clinical competencies. The first is the ability to structure a problem and identify the data needed for a solution. The second is the ability to use databases to obtain information in real-time and to use decision aids (decision support systems). In many schools, at least some of the exams are held with an open book. Examinees are not required to demonstrate whether they remember the information but if they can apply it to solve a problem. The third component is the ability to critically read clinical essays on disease diagnosis, treatment, and prognosis. This ability allows learning from the collective rather than from one's own experience.

References

Albanese MA, Mitchell S. Problem-based learning: a review of literature on its outcomes and implementation issues. Acad Med. 1993;68:52–81.
Benor D. Early clinical program for novice medical students. Isr J Med Sci. 1987;23:81–9.
Brown MEL, Anderson K, Finn GM. A narrative literature review considering the development and implementation of longitudinal integrated clerkships, including a practical guide for application. J Med Educat Curri Develop. 2019;6:1–12.
Campbell EJM. The McMaster medical School at Hamilton, Ontario. Lancet. 1970;II:763–7.
Caygill R, Peardon M, Waite C, Wright J. Comparing a longitudinal integrated clerkship with traditional hospital-based rotations in a rural setting. Med Teach. 2017;39(5):520–6.

Cohen-Schotanus J, Muijtjens AM, Schonrock-Adema J, Geertsma J, van der Vleuten CP. Effects of conventional and problem-based learning on clinical and general competencies and career development. Med Educ. 2008;42:256–65.

Donetto S. Medical students' views of power in doctor-patient interactions: the value of teacher-learner relationships. Med Educ. 2010;44:187–96.

Dube T, Schinke R, Strasser R. It takes a community to train a future physician: social support experienced by medical students during a community-engaged longitudinal integrated clerkship. Can Med Educ J. 2019;10:e5–e16.

Engel GL. The need for a new medical model. A challenge to biomedicine. Science. 1977;196:129–36.

Engel GL. How much longer must medicine's science be hound by a seventeenth century worldview? Psychother Psychosom. 1992;57:3–16.

Galen RS, Gambino SR. Beyond normality: the predictive value and efficiency of medical diagnoses. New York: Wiley; 1975.

Guyatt G, Cairns J, Churchill D, Cook D, Haynes B, Hirsh J, Irvine J, Levine M, Levine M, Nishikawa J, Sackett D. Evidence-based medicine: a new approach to teaching the practice of medicine. JAMA. 1992;268(17):2420–5.

Hartling L, Spooner C, Tjosvold L, Oswald A. Problem-based learning in pre-clinical medical education: 22 years of outcome research. Med Teach. 2010;32(1):28–35.

Hilfiker D. Making Medical Mistakes. Harper's Report 1980; 59–65.

Hirsh D, Gaufberg E, Ogur B, Cohen P, Krupat E, Cox M, Pelletier S, Bor D. Educational outcomes of the Harvard Medical School-Cambridge integrated clerkship: a way forward for medical education. Acad Med. 2012;87(5):643–50.

Kuhn T. The structure of scientific revolutions. 2nd ed. Chicago: University of Chicago Press; 1970.

Lewis AD, Menezes DA, McDermott HE, Hibbert LJ, Brennan SL, Ross EE, Jones LA. A comparison of course-related stressors in undergraduate problem-based learning (PBL) versus non-PBL medical programs. BMC Med Educ. 2009;9:60.

Ludmerer KM. Learner-centered medical education. N Engl J Med. 2004;351:1163–5.

Norris TE, Schaad DC, DeWitt D, Ogur B, Hunt DD. Consortium of longitudinal integrated clerkships. Longitudinal integrated clerkships for medical students: an innovation adopted by medical schools in Australia, Canada, South Africa, and the United States. Acad Med. 2009;84(7):902–7.

Ogrinc G, Mutha S, Irby DM. Evidence for longitudinal ambulatory care rotations: a review of the literature. Acad Med. 2002;77(7):688–93.

Perkins DN, Salomon G. Are cognitive skills context-bound? Educ Res. 1989;18:16–25.

Snow SC, Gong J, Adams JE. Faculty experience and engagement in a longitudinal integrated clerkship. Med Teach. 2017;39(5):527–34.

Teherani A, Irby DM, Loeser H. Outcomes of different clerkship models: longitudinal integrated, hybrid, and block. Acad Med. 2013;88(1):35–43.

Trullàs JC, Blay C, Sarri E, Pujol R. Effectiveness of problem-based learning methodology in undergraduate medical education: a scoping review. BMC Med Educ. 2022;22:104.

Walters L, Greenhill J, Richards J, Ward H, Campbell N, Ash J, Schuwirth LW. Outcomes of longitudinal integrated clinical placements for students, clinicians, and society. Med Educ. 2012;46(11):1028–41.

Chapter 6
Patient Care, Teaching, and Research

Abstract The task of universities is to teach. Research, however, is more enjoyable and the main criterion for prestige, promotion, and tenure. Many academics see teaching as a non-rewarding, time-consuming, and emotionally draining distraction from their research. Furthermore, teaching is not the highest priority in medical schools. Clinicians care first, for patients, second for residents, fellows, and research projects, and teaching comes last. The survival of preclinical teachers depends on their research productivity. Consequently, teaching may be done by junior faculty who cannot refuse the demands of their department chairs. This section explores the relationship between teaching and research; the need to include research methods in the curriculum; and the role of the clinician-scientist.

6.1 Assessment of Research and Teaching in Higher Education

6.1.1 Assessment of Research Productivity

Common measures of research productivity are the number of publications and citations per publication. Some institutions consider the year of publication (it takes time for citations to accumulate), type (review papers attract more citations), discipline, and the number of authors in each publication.

The assessment of research productivity is based on publications produced and grants received. Such an assessment may degrade the commitment of the university to scholarship and intellectual discourse (Macfarlane 2021). Liberal education considers philosophical reflection and intellectual engagement as "research." Scholarship, i.e., interpretation of what is already known, is the main drive for innovation in the humanities, just as experimental research is the means for innovation in the sciences. In 1986, Elton recommended a change in the assessment system of universities, giving equal value to teaching, scholarship, and research.

6.1.2 Assessment of Teaching Performance

Contrary to the assumption that teaching productivity cannot be increased, there is some evidence that teachers who receive information about their performance do improve, and it is believed that structured evaluation systems can lead to more than a temporary increase in teacher effectiveness and promote professional development (Taylor and Tyler 2012). Teaching performance is evaluated using student ratings, student debriefings, graduate student evaluations, supervisor evaluations, self-evaluations, or summative assessments based on combinations of criteria (Sandholtz and Shea 2012). These evaluations provide formative feedback to faculty and course coordinators. Measures of teaching performance also inform decisions about contract renewal, promotion, and tenure. Finally, they provide evidence of institutional efforts to ensure teaching quality (Spooren et al. 2013).

The main problem of teaching evaluation is the lack of a theoretical framework for effective teaching. Definitions of effective teaching differ within and between institutions (Spooren et al. 2013). The early studies in the 1970s indicated acceptable stability and internal consistency of student ratings. It was claimed that students' criteria for evaluation assessed the quality of the presentation of the material rather than its entertainment value. Students cited clarity and stimulation of intellectual curiosity in describing their best lecturers (Costin et al. 1971). More recent studies found a positive correlation between student ratings and other indicators of teaching quality, such as learning outcomes, graduate ratings, and self-assessments (Spooren et al. 2013). These findings encouraged faculty to use student ratings for the assessment of teaching. In many institutions, student ratings have become the sole measure of teaching effectiveness (Berk 2013), and they have been incorporated into the LCME standards for medical school accreditation.

Yet to this day, despite a plethora of subsequent studies, evaluating teaching effectiveness remains a "…thorny, vexing and tricky issue" (Berk 2013). A 2013 review of the literature since 2000 found that the validity of student ratings of teaching remains uncertain because first, teachers, students, and questionnaire designers may have different perceptions of effective teaching. Secondly, questionnaires are expected to capture several dimensions of good teaching practice. However, the lack of agreement on these dimensions has led to significant questionnaire variability. Third, there is disagreement about the nature of the weak to strong positive correlations between student ratings and student achievements on examinations. Do good ratings lead to better achievements, or does the expectation of better achievement affect ratings? Finally, the finding that ratings improve with teacher age and seniority has not been confirmed. Many teachers do not find student ratings helpful and tend to ignore student comments and suggestions.

These findings suggest that student ratings may not provide useful information to improve teaching (Spooren et al. 2013). In 2017, Hornstein argued that the use of student ratings as a basis for faculty retention and promotion decisions is misguided because, first, averages derived from categorical data (e.g., "unacceptable," "poor," "good," and "excellent") are meaningless as they are not ordinal. Second, students are not dispassionate evaluators of teaching performance: They may care about grades, while faculty care about student learning. Third, students may reliably evaluate aspects such as the instructor's audibility and availability outside of class, but not pedagogy. Fourth, to achieve the highest possible rating, some instructors may meet unreasonable student expectations (Hornstein 2017). Another compelling argument against using student ratings of individual instructors (as opposed to course ratings) is their possible association with students' cognitive development: students who expect to be taught absolute truths may evaluate instruction differently than those who expect to be challenged to reflect and choose between alternatives.

Therefore, students' ratings are insufficient to assess teaching. Even assuming that student ratings are a valid assessment of teaching, many, if not most, studies have failed to include the *amount* of teaching in that assessment. One may imagine a situation in which a brilliant academic receives higher ratings from students after a single lecture in a course consisting of 12 weekly sessions than her less brilliant colleague who teaches the remaining sessions. Therefore, students' ratings should be supplemented by additional assessment methods of teaching courses and individual faculty. For example, supervisor evaluations may identify ways to improve communication with students; student debriefing may provide information on students' specific difficulties, e.g., exams, quality of teaching, comfort in classrooms, laboratory experience, and their clinical learning environment.

6.2 Teaching and/or vs Research

Whether research and teaching support, hinder or have nothing to do with each other remains an open question, and plausible arguments can be put forward for each of these alternatives. A 1987 meta-analysis found that the correlation coefficients between research productivity and teaching quality ranged from 0.06 to 0.12 (Feldman 1987), and a later meta-analysis confirmed that the two are unrelated (Marsh and Hattie 2002).

However, some authors argue that teaching and research are mutually supportive (Keohane 1993). Teaching forces academics to clarify the background of their research, and students' comments, questions, and criticisms can suggest new directions; research keeps knowledge up to date, and encounters with people of different ages can be intellectually stimulating. Other authors argue that the demands of teaching limit the time needed for research; that sharing in research requires communication with colleagues rather than students; and that researchers need to be highly specialized while teachers need to be broad scholars. I conclude that research certainly competes with teaching for faculty time and energy. Productivity in research requires enthusiasm, creativity, and the ability to communicate—all important prerequisites for teaching, and this explains why some teachers excel in both areas.

6.3 The Case for Including Science Education in the Undergraduate Curriculum[1]

The preclinical part of the undergraduate medical curriculum aims to acquaint students with the various scientific disciplines and the methods of inquiry that define them as such; with the normal and abnormal structure and function of the human body, and with the medical terminology that would permit students communication with their clinical mentors. The clinical phase aims to familiarize students with patients with common diseases, their causes, complications, and treatment, and to provide them with the skills to communicate with patients, perform a physical examination, solve medical problems, and respond to the needs of individual patients.

Both parts of the curriculum have been criticized for overemphasizing the scientific basis of medicine, thereby directing its graduates toward academization, overspecialization, and scientific research, but not toward the needs of their patients and the humane aspects of health care. Therefore, the attempts to include science education, research methodology, or student research programs (Binneveld and Vleesenbeek 1976; Lubsen and Benbassat 1990; AAMC-HHMI Committee 2009) in the curriculum breed controversy. In this subsection, I list the arguments for including science education in the undergraduate curriculum.

6.3.1 Objectives of Science Education

The AAMC-HHMI Committee specified in their 2009 report that science education should impart to learners an ability to understand the process of scientific inquiry; explain how scientific knowledge is discovered and validated; develop observational and interpretive skills through hands-on laboratory or field experiences; to read and analyze results presented in a paper from the scientific literature; develop a hypothesis based on the results, and describe experiments that test this hypothesis (AAMC-HHMI Committee 2009).

The main argument for including science education in the curriculum is the need to teach the ability to distinguish between facts and hypotheses. Today, medical curricula include methods of laboratory-based research, but only a few include methods of population-based research. Students need to be taught an understanding of the relationship between disease manifestations and diagnosis, therapy and prognosis, and how to translate data from laboratory and population-based research into the treatment of individual patients.

Science education is *not* intended to teach students how to perform *unsupervised* research. It is intended to teach the inferential skills necessary for clinical work,

---

[1] A previous version of this section was published in Lubsen J, Benbassat J. Wetenschappelijke vorming in het medisch curriculum—noodzaak of ballast? [in Dutch] Medisch Contact 1990; 45: 1028–1030. With permission from the editor.

thus producing physicians who can critically evaluate the flood of information that comes their way daily. Physicians are expected to stay current. Medical schools would not be fulfilling their mission if their only goal was to train physicians who could practice according to the state of the art on the day they graduate.

Just as science education provides the ability to evaluate research, it also fosters the ability to evaluate personal experiences and suppresses the tendency to place too much value on one's observations. Science education also provides insight into the probabilistic aspects of clinical reasoning. Teaching Bayes' theorem can help students move from a dichotomous right/wrong view of knowledge to a realistic understanding of scientific ideas, data, and evidence by making them aware that uncertainty can be reduced but not eliminated (Rosenberg et al. 2022).

6.3.2 Similarity Between Scientific Research and Clinical Problem-Solving

The methods of scientific research duplicate inferences of diagnostic reasoning. Scientists and physicians formulate a hypothesis and ask what is the probability that it is correct. To answer this question, scientists draw inferences from research data and physicians draw inferences from the patient's history, physical examination, and ancillary tests. To this end, they both apply Bayes' rules. Physicians infer from applying tests with established sensitivity and specificity to a patient *with an estimated pre-test probability of having the hypothesized disease*. Similarly, confirmation of a scientific hypothesis requires not only a p-value (equivalent to 1—the specificity of the diagnostic test) below an arbitrary threshold but also the prior probability that the hypothesis is correct (equivalent to the pre-test probability of disease) and the statistical power of the experiment to correctly reject the null hypothesis if it is false (equivalent to the sensitivity of the test) (Pharoah 2007).

A common mistake is to consider the p-value alone as a test of the hypothesis (see Sect. 7.3). This error (the "p-value fallacy") is equivalent to considering only the specificity of the test when confirming a clinical diagnosis. The error is due to the failure to recognize that the probability of the observed findings given the hypothesis is not the same as the probability of the hypothesis given the observed findings. In 2005, Ioannidis even claimed that "most [sic!] published findings are wrong" because they ignore the prior probability that the hypothesis being tested is correct.

6.3.3 Summing Up

For all these reasons, I concur that science education, research methodology, or student research programs are worthwhile components of the undergraduate curriculum. The type of research in which students can participate is of secondary importance. For my part, I prefer patient-based research, biostatistics, and clinical epidemiology because the topics they cover are better aligned with clinical practice.

The administration and faculty can motivate medical students to engage in research. In The Netherlands, 15–20% of medical students have a published paper indexed in Pubmed on the day they graduate (van Eyk et al. 2010). A 2015 review of the literature on the research activity of medical students revealed that they had positive attitudes toward research and having it as part of the required or elective curriculum. This review also highlighted the factors that may discourage student research programs, namely, unreasonably high expectations of student participants and lack of mentorship (Chang and Ramnanan 2015). While both preclinical and clinical faculty can provide guidance and supervision in laboratory-based research, student participation in patient-oriented research projects remains limited by its interdisciplinary nature and by the availability of mentors.

6.4 Clinician-Scientists[2]

"Clinician-scientists" is an all-inclusive term for board-certified specialists who engage in patient care and laboratory-based (biomedical) research, patient-based (clinical) research, or population-based (epidemiological) research. Biomedical (laboratory-based) research is in the domain of the basic sciences, and includes T1 translational research, which is defined as "the transfer of new understandings of disease mechanisms gained in the laboratory into the development of new methods for diagnosis, therapy, and prevention." Patient-based (clinical) research includes T2 translational research, which refers to the application of results from bench studies into practice by conducting trials on the efficacy and side effects of treatment or diagnostic interventions. Population-based (epidemiological) research includes attempts to identify risk indicators of diseases, establish the association between disease manifestations and diagnosis, and between therapy and prognosis (Woolf 2008).

In recent years, the number of medical graduates who choose to combine patient care and research has declined, generating concerns about the future of medical research (O'Rahilly 2023). This subsection reviews the reasons for this decline, the interventions to reverse it, and the projections for the future role of clinician-scientists.

---

[2] An earlier version of this section was published in Baumal R, Benbassat J, Van JA. Reflections on the current and future roles of clinician-scientists. The Israel Medical Association journal: IMAJ. 2014; 16: 475–8. With permission from the editor.

6.4.1 Reasons for the Declining Numbers of Clinician-Scientists

The decline in the number of physicians who combine patient care and research occurs mostly among clinician-biomedical scientists. This decline has been blamed for the delay in the translation of laboratory breakthroughs into new clinical interventions (Roberts et al. 2012). In contrast, the amount of patient-based research has increased over the last decades, as evidenced by the increase in the number of trials that evaluate therapeutic leads discovered at the bench (Sackett 2000). Still, this increase does not appear to meet all needs. T2 translational research, which has involved as many as 60% of U.S. children with cancer, has been credited for the fourfold increase in their survival rates over recent decades. It has been suggested that this achievement may be reduplicated in other diseases by increasing the number of clinicians-epidemiologists, clinical trials, and patients involved in them (Gelijns and Gabriel 2012).

The declining numbers of medical graduates who choose careers as clinician-biomedical scientists and the growing need for clinician-scientists who engage in patient-based research have raised concerns. One possible cause for this decline is the economic constraints of the health environment. Unlike the period before 1965, today only a few teaching hospitals can afford research sections in their clinical departments (Feldman 2012), and financial pressures have eliminated the research experience from many residency programs. Constraints in salaries and support were identified as obstacles to clinical research in Canada (Donath et al. 2009).

Second, the decline in the number of clinician-biomedical scientists may be due to the changes that have occurred in undergraduate medical education. These changes have limited students' proficiency in the biomedical sciences. Because of the advances in biomedical knowledge, medical faculties can no longer provide students with a comprehensive introduction to the entire array of biomedical scientific disciplines that were the basis of the medical curriculum until the mid-1960s. In addition, the adoption of the bio-psychosocial model of medical care has resulted in the biomedical sciences having to compete with the behavioral sciences for curricular time. Finally, the transition from deductive to evidence-based reasoning has led some faculty to even question the value of teaching the basic sciences (Ling et al. 2008).

Third, the training is too long. A 2010 review of 24 North American MD-PhD programs found that, on average, they required 8 years to complete (Brass et al. 2010). Adding pre-med and residency, the training of a clinician-scientist would total 15–18 years, thereby increasing the economic burden on young physicians. Indeed, long research training was one of the main barriers to career entry that were perceived by Canadian clinician-scientists (Lander et al. 2010). All these reasons are certainly valid and worth addressing. However, since 2000, several authors have suggested an additional reason for the decline in the number of physicians reporting research as their primary career, namely, the difficulties in maintaining the dual role of clinicians and scientists.

6.4.2 Clinician-Scientists: Difficulties Maintaining the Dual Role

As early as 2000, Sackett argued that "the proportion of clinicians who identified themselves as [bio-medical scientists] ..., began to decline as the knowledge and skills they needed for success on the bench moved ever further from those they needed for competency and safety at the bedside; ... Increasingly they have been replaced by Ph.D. full-time researchers; and... their previous attractiveness as role models for medical students declined in parallel with their diminishing clinical skills, and many became more comfortable at the blackboard than at the bedside."

In a similar vein, Marks (2007) argued that "historically, [clinician]-scientists ... conducted teaching rounds in the hospital, and... were often avidly pursued as the most important sources of new knowledge... Now physician-scientists are rarely seen in the hospital; they are most often spotted at their desks tapping out yet another grant application. Most struggle to find the time to mentor students and clinical trainees, let alone to care for patients." Most participants in the 2009 survey of Canadian clinician-scientists that I quoted earlier, "found it difficult to balance the various obligations of being a staff physician with the pursuit of their research endeavors" (Donath et al. 2009). Similarly, in 2010 Schafer stated that "[T]he vast and dramatically changing bodies of knowledge in both [clinical practice and research]... have made it humanly impossible for any individual to attain even a semblance of mastery of much of it." Finally, Wilson-Kovacs and Hauskeller (2012) quoted a British clinical scientist who stated: "You're expected to do two jobs... There's no point trying to compete as a clinician because you can't ...and there's no point trying to compete as a full-blown academic scientist ... because again you can't... What you have to do is pick the important things from both areas and apply them in the middle in an attempt to bring both areas together."

6.4.3 Projections for the Future

The main reason for the declining interest in the career of a clinician-scientist is the difficulties in maintaining the dual role of a care provider and investigator. The complexities of patient care and research have made it impossible for an individual to attain mastery in both fields. It seems that rather than expecting clinician-scientists to compete with full-time clinicians in providing patient care, and with full-time investigators in performing research, clinician-scientists will increasingly assume the role of leading/coordinating interdisciplinary teams.

Such teams would focus either on patient-oriented research or on the clinical, biomedical, and epidemiological aspects of specific clinical diseases, such as hypertension and diabetes, coagulation disorders, or rheumatoid arthritis/autoimmune diseases. Multidisciplinary teams of clinicians and basic scientists would conduct epidemiologic and biomedical research, rather than working together in an ad hoc fashion (Roberts et al. 2012), with basic scientists with MD or Ph.D. degrees conducting the biomedical investigation of the particular clinical problem, and clinicians conducting research with patients. By bridging the gap between clinical practice and medical research, clinician-scientists would lead and coordinate the research. Indeed, already today, interdisciplinary research has become a priority for funding organizations (Laberge et al. 2009).

References

AAMC-HHMI Committee "Scientific foundations for future physicians." 2009. https://www.aamc.org/system/files?file=2020-02/scientificfoundationsforfuturephysicians.pdf. Accessed Sept 2023.
Berk RA. Top five flashpoints in the assessment of teaching effectiveness. Med Teach. 2013;35(1):15–26.
Binneveld JMW, Vleesenbeek HH. Medische Faculteit Rotterdam: analyse van een experiment. Leiden: Stenfert Kroese; 1976.
Brass LF, Akabas MH, Burnley LD, Engman DM, Wiley CA, Andersen OS. Are MD-PhD programs meeting their goals? An analysis of career choices made by graduates of 24 MD-PhD programs. Acad Med. 2010;85:692–701.
Chang Y, Ramnanan CJ. A review of literature on medical students and scholarly research: experiences, attitudes, and outcomes. Acad Med. 2015;90(8):1162–73.
Costin F, Greenough WT, Menges RJ. Student ratings of college teaching: reliability, validity, and usefulness. Rev Educ Res. 1971;41(5):511–35.
Donath E, Filion KB, Eisenberg MJ. Improving the clinician-scientist pathway: a survey of clinician-scientists. Arch Intern Med. 2009;169:1242–4.
Elton L. Research and teaching: Symbiosis or conflict. High Educ. 1986;15:299–304.
Feldman KA. Research productivity and scholarly accomplishment of college teachers as related to their instructional effectiveness: a review and exploration. Res High Educ. 1987;26:227–98.
Feldman AM. Mortgaging the future of medical research. Clin Transl Sci. 2012;5:113–4.
Gelijns AC, Gabriel SE. Looking beyond translation—integrating clinical research with medical practice. N Engl J Med. 2012;366:1659–61.
Hornstein HA. Student evaluations of teaching are inadequate assessment tool for evaluating faculty performance. Cogent Education. 2017;4(1):1304016.
Ioannidis JPA. Why most published research findings are false. PLoS Med. 2005;2:e124.
Keohane NO. The Mission of the research university. Deadalus. 1993;122:101–25.
Laberge S, Albert M, Hodges BD. Perspectives of clinician and biomedical scientists on interdisciplinary health research. CMAJ. 2009;181:797–803.
Lander B, Hanley GE, Atkinson-Grosjean J. Clinician-scientists in Canada: barriers to career entry and progress. PLoS One. 2010;5(10):e13168.
Ling Y, Swanson DB, Holtzman K, Bucak SD. Retention of basic science information by senior medical students. Acad Med. 2008;83:S82–5.
Lubsen J, Benbassat J. Wetenschappelijke vorming in het medisch curriculum—noodzaak of ballast? [in Dutch]. Medisch Contact. 1990;45:1028–30.
Macfarlane B. The spirit of research. Oxf Rev Educ. 2021;47(6):737–51.
Marks AR. Physician-scientist, heal thyself. J Clin Invest. 2007;117:2.
Marsh HW, Hattie J. The relation between research productivity and teaching effectiveness: complementary, antagonistic, or independent constructs? J High Educ. 2002;73(5):603–41.
O'Rahilly S. Academic clinician–scientists risk becoming an endangered species. Nat Med. 2023;29:1–1.

Pharoah P. How not to interpret a P-value? JNCI. 2007;99:332–3.

Roberts SF, Fischhoff MA, Sakowski SA, Feldman EL. Perspective: Transforming science into medicine: how clinician-scientists can build bridges across research's "valley of death". Acad Med. 2012;87:266–70.

Rosenberg JM, Kubsch M, Wagenmakers EJ, Dogucu M. Making sense of uncertainty in the science classroom. Sci & Educ. 2022;14:1–24.

Sackett DL. The fall of "clinical research" and the rise of "clinical-practice research". Clin Invest Med. 2000;23:331–3.

Sandholtz JH, Shea LM. Predicting performance: a comparison of university supervisors' predictions and teacher candidates' scores on a teaching performance assessment. J Teach Educ. 2012;63(1):39–50.

Schafer AI. The vanishing physician-scientist? Trans Res. 2010;155:1–2.

Spooren P, Brockx B, Mortelmans D. On the validity of student evaluation of teaching: the state of the art. Rev Educ Res. 2013;83(4):598–642.

Taylor ES, Tyler JH. The effect of evaluation on teacher performance. Am Econ Rev. 2012;102(7):3628–51.

van Eyk HJ, Hooiveld MHW, van Leeuwen TN, van der Wurff BLJ, de AJM C, Dekker FW. Scientific output of Dutch medical students. Med Teach. 2010;32:231–5.

Wilson-Kovacs DM, Hauskeller C. The clinician-scientist: professional dynamics in clinical stem cell research. Sociol Health Illn. 2012;34(4):497–512.

Woolf SH. The meaning of translational research and why it matters. JAMA. 2008;299:211–3.

Chapter 7
Social Influences on Education, Research, and Healthcare

Abstract The concepts of belief and knowledge, and their implications for research are controversial. Beliefs become knowledge when supported by evidence, and evidence has different levels of credibility. This section will briefly define the terms objectivism and relativism; describe the levels of credibility of evidence; and the current, desirable, and undesirable social influences on knowledge. I shall argue that research is guided by the choice of hypotheses to be confirmed; that this choice depends on the researcher's belief that the hypothesis is correct; and that society's culture determines this belief.

7.1 Objectivism and Relativism

In 1976, Bernstein (cited by Bloland 1990) distinguished between the paradigms of objectivism and relativism. Objectivism is the belief in a framework to which one can appeal to determine rationality, knowledge, truth, or rightness. Relativism denies the possibility of such a framework. It maintains that the concepts of belief and knowledge must be understood relative to the current culture of society and that prevailing beliefs define knowledge. In other words, relativism posits that education and knowledge acquisition are socially determined.

In 1981, Clark (1981) referred to these two seemingly incompatible paradigms. On the one hand, logic, mathematics, or any subject matter are universal rather than property of any culture. Therefore, the premise that knowledge is socially determined is irrational as it makes it a matter for bargaining. Accepting that knowledge is socially determined would destroy the educational enterprise, as it would consist of imposing views and attempts at dominance. On the other hand, it is unclear why certain truths are established at one time rather than another, why a particular knowledge is selected as worthy of education, and how certain selections from a corpus of truths become adopted for curricula. Sociologists of knowledge must explore such influences so that we can guard against them (Clark 1981).

7.2 Levels of Scientific Evidence

Knowledge is the conviction that something is true. To believe that something is true, people rely on evidence. To justify belief, the evidence must meet certain standards (Clark 1981). Questions such as "What is the line that separates knowledge and belief?" are fundamental to education and research (Southerland et al. 2001) and particularly relevant to medical practice.

Since the 1980s, there have been repeated efforts to define the different levels of evidence for the effectiveness of medical interventions. in 1992, Guyatt et al. coined the term "evidence-based medicine" (EBM) in contrast to medicine based on pathophysiological reasoning or personal, non-systematic experience. EBM comprises a hierarchy that places meta-analyses and systematic reviews of randomized controlled trials (RCTs) at the highest level of evidence, cohort studies, case-control studies, and cross-sectional studies at an intermediate level, and case series and expert opinion at the lowest level of evidence. EBM recognizes that clinical practice cannot be limited to interventions supported by the highest level of evidence and that, in the absence of RCTs, doctors must use interventions with lower-level evidence of effectiveness. Furthermore, not all RCTs are properly conducted or reported in terms of randomization, blinding, number of subjects withdrawn from the study, confidence intervals around study estimates, and power analysis (Howick 2011; Burns et al. 2011).

Since its introduction, EBM) has dominated medical practice, teaching, and policy. However, EBM is also subject to criticism. First, it addresses different issues in clinical practice, and the evidence needs to be adjusted depending on whether it relates to treatment, prognosis, diagnosis, or economic analysis. For example, RCTs are not appropriate when it comes to the prognosis of a disease (Burns et al. 2011). Second, EBM limits the role of basic research in patient treatment, and it has been argued that both population and laboratory research are needed to understand the causes of disease (La Caze 2011). Third, policymakers have used EBM to support clinical guidelines that are opposed by some clinicians (Howick 2011).

These criticisms suggest that EBM) needs to be further developed and improved. Still, I believe that EBM provides a better basis for medical decision-making than the personal experience and pathophysiologic rationale that dominated practice before the introduction of EBM in 1992.

7.3 Social Influences on Knowledge and Beliefs

7.3.1 Social Influences on Research

How can we explain why certain truths are established at one time rather than another and the impact of social beliefs on scientific inquiry? In Chap. 6, I referred to the "p-value fallacy" in the interpretation of the findings of scientific research, and to the importance of recognizing that the probability of the observed findings given the hypothesis *is not the same* as the probability of the hypothesis given the observed findings. To answer the question "What is the probability that the hypothesis is correct given the observed findings?" it is not sufficient to know only the p-value. One must also consider first, the statistical power of the experiment to correctly reject the null hypothesis if it is false, and second, the prior probability that the hypothesis is correct. *This prior probability is the subjective estimate of the researcher. It is reasonable to assume that the mere choice to test a specific hypothesis is due to the belief of the researcher that it is correct, and that this estimate, in turn, is guided by the prevailing social beliefs.* So how can we reduce the impact of social beliefs on research? I feel that this can be achieved by closer scrutiny of unexpected results of empirical studies. The history of science is replete with unexpected observations that led to a paradigm shift in reasoning. Although casual observations and unexpected research findings are not definitive evidence of cause-effect relationships, such observations should be viewed as generating hypotheses that must be confirmed by separate studies.

7.3.2 Social Influences on Health Care

Focus groups conducted in a medical center in the United States have shown that different stakeholders have different perspectives. Patients strive for respectful and caring treatment; directors struggle with allocating resources across services; physicians struggle with the impact of resource scarcity on the quality of patient care (Foglia et al. 2009). A fourth factor is the perspective of society that politicians commonly represent.

In recent decades, changes in the structure and financing of health care have led to a focus on the relationship between medicine and society. In 1982, Starr (cited by Cruess and Cruess 2020) suggested that this relationship is contractual. Since then, this "social contract" has evolved into explicit obligations and expectations on the part of both society and medicine. Society expects the healer's competence, morality, accountability, objective advice, and commitment to the common good. Medicine's expectations of society are trust, autonomy, self-regulation, an adequately funded healthcare system, shared responsibility for health, and non-financial and financial rewards.

The social effect on medical care may be a desirable response to rational, evidence-based medical needs assessment. However, reasonable patients may have unreasonable expectations and demands. Rarely, there are also cases where society's expectations and demands are controversial. Differing interpretations of these expectations have led to the variability of admission criteria to medical schools, of clinical practice between and within countries, and of government funding of health care.

The role of politics in public health is complex (Bambra et al. 2005). On the one hand, politicians ensure the financing of health care (Frenk and Donabedian 1987).

Social determinants of health, such as income inequality, housing, and education are sensitive to policy decisions (Pickett and Wilkinson 2015; Butler 2023). Populations in countries with higher public spending and lower income inequality have better access to healthcare, better self-rated health, and lower mortality (McCartney et al. 2019). On the other hand, to win elections, political parties often claim to care about the common good.[1] But once in office, politicians prioritize goals set by coalition agreements, sectoral activists, lobby groups, or campaign donors. People in general, and politicians who are aware of their power in particular, tend to be overconfident, ignore advice, pay less attention to their surroundings, and be less motivated to understand how other people think and feel (Fast et al. 2012; Hogeveen et al. 2014). This can lead to decisions serving the interests of small groups or even personal gain rather than the population. Decisions made behind closed doors are claimed to be based on expert judgment; however, politicians may manipulate knowledge, and scientists who advise political leaders risk being used in ways they cannot control (Gesser-Edelsburg et al. 2021).

Political interference has been observed in other professions such as statistics (Prevost 2019), banking (Shen and Lin 2012), law (Nielson 2010), and education (Amutabi 2003). The undesirable impact of political interference in professional matters is particularly relevant to public health. Examples of the impact of political power on public health include the US Supreme Court decisions on abortion and gun sales (Gostin and Wetter 2023) and the repeal of the tax on sweetened beverages in Israel (Troen et al. 2023). Additional damage to the healthcare system is caused by politicians issuing orders to practitioners without listening to the concerns of frontline staff (Murthy 2022). Healthcare providers who disobey a directive from their superiors may face administrative sanctions or other forms of intimidation. The result of such a high-profile battle is that healthcare providers will learn not to speak out when confronted with something unjust. This lesson will further promote moral suffering, burnout, and a culture of non-disclosure to the detriment of providers and patients.

7.4 Complementary/Alternative Medicine[2]

Medical education, practice, and research follow the biomedical model (BM) (Chaps. 2 and 5). However, in addition to BM, there are other models of clinical practices commonly referred to as complementary/alternative medicine (CAM). CAM is an all-inclusive term for clinical interventions based on theories about disease causation and treatment that differ from BM and each other in their

---

[1] I am grateful to Dr. Mayer Brezis for suggesting the possible undesirable effect of political interventions on professional issues.

[2] An earlier version of this section was published in Benbassat J. Inferences from unexpected findings of scientific research: Common misconceptions. European Journal of Integrative Medicine. 2016 Jun 1;8(3):188–90. With permission through Copyright Clearance Center.

assumptions. CAM treatments use spiritual (mental strength, prayer), nutritional (herbs, vitamins in doses not acceptable in BM), medication (homeopathy), physical (massage, chiropractic, acupuncture), or unclassifiable (iridology, aromatic therapy, reflexology) therapies. This subsection refers to another social influence on health care: the utilization of CAM.

7.4.1 Utilization of Complementary and Alternative Medicine

Surveys have revealed significant utilization of CAM in Australia, Canada, and Finland (Harris and Rees 2000). A UK survey found that 16% of the responders had seen a CAM practitioner. Women and people with higher socioeconomic status were more likely to access CAM. Musculoskeletal conditions accounted for 68% of use, and mental health for 12%. Most were through self-referral (70%) and self-financing (Sharp et al. 2018). A European study found that as many as 25.9% of the population had used CAM during the last 12 months. Typically, they used only one CAM treatment as a complementary rather than alternative treatment. The use of CAM varied from 10% in Hungary to almost 40% in Germany. The health profiles of users of CAM modalities varied and CAM use was more common among women and those with higher education (Kemppainen et al. 2018). A 1995 review found that BM doctors in Europe and the United States believe that CAM is moderately beneficial with an average efficacy score of 46 (± 18) on a scale of 1 to 100 (Ernst et al. 1995).

The main appeal of CAM is its declared aim to strengthen the vitality of the entire body and to improve the patient's ability to cope with illness. CAM offers simple explanations and a theoretical template that focuses on the patient's individual experience, rather that of groups of patients. Its language does not include probabilities. Most branches of CAM encourage patients to trust the benevolent nature and its remedies are perceived as harmless. CAM offers more than physical and mental health: it is a kind of cult that strives for a victory of spirituality over bodily diseases.

The high prevalence of utilization of CAM has led some sociologists (e.g., Shuval and Averbuch 2012) to suggest that the medical BM establishment feels challenged by CAM; that the absence of teaching of CAM in medical schools, and of governmental control on CAM aims at perpetuating the dominance of BM; and that public confidence in BM may further decline thus increasing the utilization of CAM in the future. It would appear to me that these suggestions are wrong. First, in Israel, about 1.7 million visits to CAM practitioners are estimated to occur annually, while the number of visits to BM family doctors, general practitioners, or specialists exceeds 53 million, in addition to 1.4 million hospital discharges (Israel Central Bureau of Statistics 2011). In most cases, patients do not abandon BM but turn to CAM as an additional mode of care. Second, the absence of teaching CAM in medical schools and governmental control of CAM is mostly due to difficulties in coping with the large number of CAM modalities and their theoretical bases. It would be difficult to justify a CAM teaching course within the restricted curricular schedule, whether it should include a sample or all CAM disciplines, the level of familiarity with CAM that would be expected from medical students, and the professional background of the teachers. Considering the number of CAM modalities and the poor evidence for their efficacy, it would be difficult to implement governmental control on its practitioners. Finally, the suggestion that public confidence in BM may further decline is at odds with the results of surveys in Israel that attest to stable satisfaction rates from the BM health care services that exceed 88% (Brammli-Greenberg and Medina-Artom 2015). Therefore, I believe that the BM will continue to shoulder the responsibility for patient care, and I doubt that CAM will ever be considered an alternative to biomedicine.

Both CAM and BM attempt to provide patient-centered care and may inadvertently harm patients. The claim that CAM is less expensive than conventional medical treatment is false, as in most cases CAM complements rather than replaces BM treatment (White and Ernst 2000). Like BM, the various CAM modalities are based on theoretical models with their logic. Like BM, CAM is evolving—today's homeopathy and acupuncture differ from those of the past, and chiropractic no longer claims to have solutions for all ailments. Both BM and CAM strive to test the effectiveness of their interventions through controlled trials, and the quality of their research is steadily improving (Bloom et al. 2000). However, investigation of both BM and CAM interventions must overcome the problem of the p-value fallacy.

7.4.2 The p-Value Fallacy

Some controlled trials testing the efficacy of certain CAM interventions have indicated that the probability of the observed findings given the null hypothesis is less than the p threshold of 0.05. For example, controlled trials have supported the efficacy of chiropractic for low-back pain (Walker et al. 2010) and acupuncture for blood pressure (Li et al. 2014). Should these findings be interpreted as confirming the efficacy of CAM interventions?

In Chap. 6 and Sect. 7.2, I discussed the "p-value fallacy." It is due to the failure to recognize that *the probability of the observed results given the hypothesis is not the same as the probability of the hypothesis given the observed results*. To assess the probability that the hypothesis is correct given the observed results, it is not enough to know only the p-value, just as it is not enough to know only the specificity of a diagnostic test. Bayesian rules of inference also require estimates of the statistical power of the experiment to reject the null hypothesis if it is false and the prior probability that the hypothesis being tested is correct. In other words, the interpretation of trials of clinical interventions requires an estimate before the trial of the likelihood that the treatment is effective.

The CAM controversy is partly due to different assessments of the prior likelihood of the hypothesis being tested. Proponents of BM would assess this probability as low because the treatment is incompatible with scientific BM notions;

therefore, they would ignore research findings that suggest such a benefit. Proponents of CAM would assess this probability as high because it is consistent with their theory of disease: therefore, they would interpret positive trial results as proof of efficacy.

Should findings indicating that CAM treatments are efficacious be ignored because of their low prior probability? The history of medicine abounds with unexpected observations that led to paradigmatic shifts in clinical reasoning. For example, contrary to the then prevailing BM belief, treatment with quinidine was found to *increase* mortality in patients with arrhythmias, and treatment with beta-blockers was found to *improve* left ventricular function. Contrary to the BM premise that disease is the consequence of structural or biochemical disorders, the observed associations between life events and morbidity, and between socioeconomic status and mortality led to the acceptance of psycho-social predictors of disease.

Therefore, observed incompatibilities between theory and practice should prompt further inquiry. Chance observations, unexpected research findings, and positive findings of trials testing hypotheses with very low prior probabilities do not provide definitive evidence for cause-effect relationships. However, such observations *generate* hypotheses to be confirmed by independent controlled trials. BM may benefit from findings suggesting the efficacy of CAM treatments. Even when such findings do not *confirm* the worth of CAM treatment, they *generate* credible hypotheses that should be further explored. If CAM practitioners want to be accepted by the BM mainstream, they should seek such confirmatory evidence by careful, statistically sound, controlled trials.

Proponents of CAM argue that population-based randomized trials cannot assess CAM practices that view illness within the context of a particular individual (Tonelli and Callahan 2001). Therefore, a second way to examine CAM interventions is by n-of-1 controlled trials (Lillie et al. 2011). A patient is assigned to receive a sequence of CAM and control interventions, in a random order. If the patient's problem disappears during the CAM treatment, it can be established that it is effective. N-of-1 trials are consistent with claims that the assessment of the efficacy of CAM practices should be made within the context of a particular individual only (Tonelli and Callahan 2001), and the Oxford Centre for EBM ranked such trials as Level 1 evidence for treatment decision in individual patients (Howick 2011). Therefore, I believe that future research on the efficacy of CAM will focus on n-of-1 rather than on population-based clinical trials.

7.4.3 Conclusions

Four features appear to distinguish between CAM and BM. First, CAM practitioners avoid judgmental attitudes toward patients and do not differentiate between objective findings and subjective experience. A CAM therapist is not likely to say that the patient's complaints are the product of his/her imagination. Second, BM is less optimistic, more realistic, more likely to share information with patients about their illness, and less likely to promote false illusions. Third, while BM care providers assume responsibility for the treatment, CAM practitioners view themselves as mere facilitators of patients' self-healing. Most CAM theories assume that the cause of the disease and the ability to treat it are within the patient, and failure of CAM therapy is attributed to the patient's inability to believe in the value of the treatment or to keep negative thoughts away from his mind.

The fourth difference is the main one: BM has succeeded in preventing disease by vaccination and finding therapies such as insulin for diabetes, antibiotics for bacterial infections, treatment of high blood pressure, and antiviral medicines. None of the CAM professions has produced similar breakthroughs. Furthermore, assumptions like those of homeopathy that the dilutions of a substance have a biological effect, violate the laws of physics and chemistry.

It seems that these differences justify four conclusions regarding the status of CAM. The first one stems from the evidence that the use of some CAM therapies was associated with kidney failure (Vanherweghem et al. 1993) or lead poisoning (Beigel et al. 1998). This necessitates supervision of their sale to the public. Second, selective recognition of some CAM professions should be abolished. Currently, chiropractic and acupuncture are licensed in many countries, while most CAM modalities are not. Selective recognition may mislead society into believing that some CAM remedies are more useful than others. Today there is no justification to permit the practice of psychoanalysis, acupuncture, chiropractic, and astrology and to prohibit the practice of iridology, reflexology, and homeopathy.

I am aware that placing psychoanalysis, homeopathy, astrology, and acupuncture in the same category may alienate both the BM and CAM establishment. However, they are all based on unproven assumptions and anecdotal observations. Their validity may be proven in the future by conventional scientific methods. Until then, their use is based on personal belief. I for one, believe in psychoanalysis although I am aware that its efficacy has not been proven. I expect others to respect my belief in psychoanalysis, just as I recognize the beliefs of others in treatment methods of unproven efficacy.

Third, I suggest that all CAM practices should be permitted by law. However, such a sweeping permit would create a dilemma between respecting the autonomy of the individual to choose his/her health provider and protecting public health by supervising all CAM professions. The fourth conclusion is that the foundation of both BM and CAM practices on evidence should be encouraged. Today, CAM is in a stage of self-examination like that which began in BM in the 1940s with the beginning of controlled trials to test the effectiveness of clinical interventions. It took 40 years between the beginning of clinical trials and the efforts to base clinical practice on evidence; I believe that CAM will also abandon unhelpful interventions in the future.

Therefore, my attitude to CAM is ambivalent. On the one hand, I agree that the use of CAM is an important social process that should be subject to scientific scrutiny; that respecting a patient's autonomy supports an individual's right to select a healthcare provider for his/her choice, and that BM practitioners should strive to emulate the mutual trust that characterizes the relationship between patients and

CAM practitioners. On the other hand, while both BM and CAM abound with anecdotal reports of individual successes, only BM can claim to have breakthrough treatment modalities that I referred to earlier. I cannot envisage how to design an effective governmental control on the quality of CAM care, and which government agency should implement this control. Finally, the ethical principle of fair distribution of health resources implies that the health care system cannot provide free-of-charge CAM services of mostly unproven or untested efficacy, and still exclude from the package of benefits medications and technology of proven efficacy because of their cost.

References

Amutabi MN. Political interference in the running of education in post-independence Kenya: a critical retrospection. Int J Educ Dev. 2003;23:127–44.
Bambra C, Fox D, Scott-Samuel A. Towards a politics of health. Health Promot Int. 2005;20:187–93.
Beigel Y, Ostfeld I, Schoenfeld N. Clinical problem-solving. A leading question. N Engl J Med. 1998;339:827–30.
Bloland HG. Higher education and high anxiety. J High Educ. 1990;18:68–73.
Bloom BS, Retbi A, Dahan S, Jonsson E. Evaluation of randomized controlled trials on complementary and alternative medicine. Int J Technol Assess Health Care. 2000;16:13–21.
Brammli-Greenberg S, Medina-Artom T. Public opinion on the level of service and performance of the healthcare system in 2014 and comparison with 2012. Jerusalem: Myers-JDC-Brookdale; 2015.
Burns PB, Rohrich RJ, Chung KC. The levels of evidence and their role in evidence-based medicine. Plast Reconstr Surg. 2011;128(1):305.
Butler SM. Why a divided new US congress will not stall action on social determinants of health. JAMA Health Forum. 2023;4:e225544–4.
Clark C. The sociology of knowledge: what it is and what it is not. Oxf Rev Educ. 1981;7:145–55.
Cruess RL, Cruess SR. Professionalism, communities of practice, and medicine's social contract. J Am Board Fam Med. 2020;33(Supplement):S50–6.
Ernst E, Resch KL, White AR. Complementary medicine. What physicians think of it: a meta-analysis. Arch Intern Med. 1995;155:2405–8.
Fast NJ, Sivanathan N, Mayer ND, Galinsky AD. Power and overconfident decision-making. Organ Behav Hum Decis Process. 2012;117:249–60.
Foglia MB, Pearlman RA, Bottrell M, Altemose JK, Fox E. Ethical challenges within veterans administration healthcare facilities: perspectives of organization leaders, clinicians, patients, and ethics committee chairpersons. Am J Bioeth. 2009;9(4):28–36.
Frenk J, Donabedian A. State intervention in medical care: types, trends and variables. Health Policy Plan. 1987;2:17–31.
Gesser-Edelsburg A, Zemach M, Hijazi R. Who are the "real" experts? The debate surrounding COVID-19 health risk management: an Israeli case study. Risk Manag Healthc Policy. 2021;14:2553–69.
Gostin LO, Wetter S. The supreme court is harming public health and the environment. JAMA. 2023;329(18):1549–50.
Guyatt G, Cairns J, Churchill D, Cook D, Haynes B, Hirsh J, Irvine J, Levine M, Levine M, Nishikawa J, Sackett D. Evidence-based medicine: a new approach to teaching the practice of medicine. JAMA. 1992;268(17):2420–5.
Harris P, Rees R. The prevalence of complementary and alternative medicine use among the general population: a systematic review of the literature. Complement Ther Med. 2000;8:88–96.

Hogeveen J, Inzlicht M, Obhi SS. Power changes how the brain responds to others. J Exp Psychol Gen. 2014;143:755–62.

Howick J. The philosophy of evidence-based medicine. New York: Wiley; 2011. Philosophy_of_Evidence-Based_Medicine20161124-21936-ml9ks9-libre.pdf.(d1wqtxts1xzle7.cloudfront.net). Accessed Oct 2023.

Israel Central Bureau of Statistics. 2011. http://tinyurl.com/cxb2hmm. Accessed 12 May 2012.

Kemppainen LM, Kemppainen TT, Reippainen JA, Salmenniemi ST, Vuolanto PH. Use of complementary and alternative medicine in Europe: health-related and sociodemographic determinants. Scand J Public Health. 2018;46(4):448–55.

La Caze A. The role of basic science in evidence-based medicine. Biol Philos. 2011;26:81–98.

Li DZ, Zhou Y, Yang YN, Ma YT, Li XM, Yu J, Zhao Y, Zhai H, Lao L. Acupuncture for essential hypertension: a meta-analysis of randomized sham-controlled clinical trials. Evid Based Complement Alternat Med. 2014;2014:279478.

Lillie EO, Patay P, Diamant J, Isell B, Topol EJ, Schork NJ. The n-of-1 clinical trial: the ultimate strategy for individualizing medicine? Per Med. 2011;8:161–73.

McCartney G, Hearty W, Arnot J, Popham F, Cumbers A, McMaster R. Impact of political economy on population health: a systematic review of reviews. Am J Public Health. 2019;109:e1–2.

Murthy VH. Confronting health worker burnout and Well-being. N Engl J Med. 2022;387:577–9.

Nielson E. Hybrid international criminal tribunals: political interference and judicial Independence. UCLA J Int'l L Foreign Aff. 2010;15:289.

Pickett KE, Wilkinson RG. Income inequality and health: a causal review. Soc Sci Med. 2015;128:316–26.

Prevost JG. Varieties of interference and protection from interference in official statistics. 2019. https://www.europarl.europa.eu/cmsdata/163746/Prevost.pdf. Accessed Jan 2023.

Sharp D, Lorenc A, Morris R, Feder G, Little P, Hollinghurst S, Mercer SW, MacPherson H. Complementary medicine use, views, and experiences: a national survey in England. BJGP Open. 2018;2(4):bjgpopen18X101614.

Shen CH, Lin CY. Why government banks underperform: a political interference view. J Financ Intermed. 2012;21(2):181–202.

Shuval J, Averbuch E. Complementary and alternative health care in Israel. Isr J Health Policy Res. 2012;1:7.

Southerland SA, Sinatra GM, Matthews MR. Belief, knowledge, and science education. Educ Psychol Rev. 2001;13:325–51.

Starr P. The social transformation of American medicine. New York: Basic Books; 1982. As quoted by Cruess.

Tonelli MR, Callahan TC. Why alternative medicine cannot be evidence-based. Acad Med. 2001;76:1213–20.

Troen I, Fink CK, Hahn P. The International Context of the Establishment of the State of Israel. 136th Annual Meeting (January 5-8, 2023), AHA; 2023.

Vanherweghem JL, Depierreux M, Tielemans C, Abramowicz D, Data M, Jadoul M, Richard C, Vandervelde D, Verbeelen D, Vanhaelen-Fastre R. Rapidly progressive interstitial renal fibrosis in young women: association with slimming regimen including Chinese herbs. Lancet. 1993;341:387–91.

Walker BF, French SD, Grant W, Green S. Combined chiropractic interventions for low-back pain. Cochrane Database Syst Rev. 2010;4:CD005427.

White AR, Ernst E. Economic analysis of complementary medicine: a systematic review. Complement Ther Med. 2000;8:111–8.

Chapter 8
Often Neglected Guidelines for Clinical Practice, Teaching, and Further Inquiry

Abstract The guidelines in this section have been extensively discussed in the past and are included to varying extents in the undergraduate medical curricula. Still, some of them seem to be ignored in clinical practice and teaching, and their re-emphasis may improve medical care.

The neglected guidelines for clinical practice are, firstly, the need to identify the patient's perceptions, concerns, and expectations. Clinicians can enhance their ability to help by making the patient's main concern, rather than the chief complaint, the starting point for patient management. Second: Rather than being offended when patients seek a second opinion, a doctor should encourage it and schedule a follow-up appointment to deal with possible discrepancies between the first and second opinions, answer the patient's questions, and provide information. Third, keep in mind that underprivileged patients are at higher risk for morbidity. Mental health problems, mental illness, drug addiction, loneliness, social isolation, and life events are associated with higher overall mortality and morbidity.

The neglected guidelines for instruction are, first, teaching basic clinical skills and patient counseling for mastery. Rather than expecting basic clinical skills to improve through repeated reinforcement during clerkship, students would be better served by a single program aimed at teaching patient interviewing, physical examination, self-directed learning, and patient counseling at a level of competency expected of a practicing physician. Secondly, tutors should caution students against unthinkingly imitating role models. No person always exhibits all the characteristics of the ideal clinician. Therefore, students should differentiate between behaviors and not between role models. Thirdly, tutors should promote students' awareness of medical errors and doctors' reactions to having committed the error. I suggest including the second victim syndrome in the undergraduate medical curriculum. Students who participate in these programs can receive counseling in an atmosphere where they are not judged but supported as they think about their future careers. Fourth, tutors should communicate to interns and residents that professional hardships are common and not due to individual shortcomings. By setting realistic expectations for medical students, tutors can reduce future stress.

8.1 Neglected Guidelines for Clinical Practice

8.1.1 Identify the Patient's Concerns and Expectations

Patients encounter a physician with a belief system that influences their understanding of, and response to advice. This system consists of ideas, concerns, and expectations (ICE). Ideas are thoughts about the complaint. Concerns are fears about its effects. Expectations refer to prescriptions, tests, referrals, patient involvement in treatment, and information about his/her condition. Patient-centered medicine requires insight into the patient's ICE.

Some patients make their ICE clear, but many leave their concerns unspoken (Suchman et al. 1997). Most commonly, patients are concerned about the impact of their disease on their well-being, function, social status, and life expectancy. They expect their physician to address the specifics of their case and are disappointed when he or she cites only prognostic statistics (Goldman et al. 2009). They may not report certain complaints (e.g., impotence, depression) because they believe that nothing can be done, because they are embarrassed, or because they fear that their suspicions will be confirmed. Others may not tell the doctor they do not want the recommended treatment because of side effects, cost, impact on lifestyle, or disbelief in its effectiveness. Still others may fear they will offend their doctor if they ask for a second medical opinion, unorthodox treatment, sick leave, or charity support.

The patient's concerns are not necessarily the same as the chief complaint. For example, a complaint of "chest pain for three months" may also be the patient's chief concern. However, the patient's expectation may be to obtain from the physician a second opinion about the need for bypass surgery. The advantage of identifying the patient's concerns is that they include all possible causes of discomfort, whereas the chief complaint is limited to symptoms and signs. An insight into the patient's concerns is also the beginning of the multistep process of empathy, in which the physician's awareness of the patient's concerns triggers a sequence of emotional engagement, compassion, and a desire to help.

Physicians can encourage patients to share their ICE by expressing a willingness to listen. In some cases, this is enough. However, patients often tend to give hints. In some cases, physicians were observed to acknowledge the hint. In most cases, however, they ignored the hints and returned to diagnostic exploration of symptoms (Ospina et al. 2019). Physicians can gain insight into the patient's ICE by asking questions such as "Does [your complaint] interfere with your daily activities or wake you up at night?," "It would help me counsel you if you tell me what *you* think about your condition," "what worries you most?" "What do you most want to avoid," or "what do you expect from treatment?" *Doctors can expand their ability to help by making the main concern, rather than the chief complaint, the starting point for patient management.*

8.1.2 Encourage Patients to Seek a Second Opinion

Discrepancies between expert opinions are worryingly common (Benbassat 2019). Therefore, it is widely agreed that patients have a right to a second opinion unless it delays a life-saving procedure. Where opinions differ, they have the right to seek advice and choose the option they believe best suits their preferences (Tosteson et al. 2018). Second opinions confirmed the original diagnosis or treatment in 43–82% of cases and led to changes in diagnosis, treatment, or prognosis in 12–69% of cases (Ruetters et al. 2016). It is therefore recommended to support patients in obtaining second opinions, suggest specialists for their specific problem, and provide tools to reconcile divergent opinions. However, to date, seeking a second opinion is usually initiated by the patient, with older patients and patients of low socioeconomic status less likely to seek a second opinion (Hillen et al. 2017). *Rather than being offended when patients seek a second opinion, a physician should encourage them to do so and schedule a follow-up appointment to help them deal with potential discrepancies between first and second opinions, answer patients' questions, and provide information.*

8.1.3 Underprivileged Patients Are at Higher Risk for Morbidity

Western medicine distinguishes between illness (the patient's perception of being ill) and disease (observable abnormalities). Patients without disease are viewed negatively. Their illness is considered a "functional disorder." "Functional" is used interchangeably with psychogenic, unexplained, and non-organic disorders. Some clinicians unconsciously adhering to stereotypes, tend to dismiss as functional the complaints of patients with mental health problems, recent life events, loneliness, low socioeconomic status, substance dependence, and belonging to an ethnic minority. This tendency is at odds with the evidence. Age, low socioeconomic status, recent life events, drug dependence, mental illness, high body mass index, and belonging to an ethnic minority are risk indicators for disease rather than for its absence.

Mental health problems (Rodgers et al. 2021), *mental illness* (Lee et al. 2020), *drug dependence* (Glei and Preston 2020), *loneliness, and social isolation* (Rico-Uribe et al. 2018) are associated with all-cause mortality. *Life events* are associated with morbidity (Holmes and Rahe 1967; Kark et al. 1995), and despite criticism of some aspects of Holmes and Rahe's experiment, it is considered evidence that life events are a nonspecific risk factor for disease (Noone 2017).

Low socioeconomic status is associated with increased morbidity and mortality (Antonovsky 1967), even after adjustment for alcohol consumption, obesity, diabetes, hypertension, physical inactivity, and smoking (Stringhini et al. 2017). *African Americans* have higher mortality rates than whites for most leading causes of death (heart disease, cancer, stroke, diabetes, kidney disease, hypertension, cirrhosis, and homicide), with a difference in life expectancy of 7 years in 1960 and 5 years in 2005, even after accounting for socioeconomic status (Williams and Mohammed 2009).

Medical educators try to counter the tendency to dismiss the symptoms of underprivileged patients by getting physicians to treat such patients like any other patient. This approach is incorrect. *Underprivileged patients are NOT like any other patient: They are at HIGHER risk for morbidity and mortality. Any symptom in a child from a dysfunctional family, in a poor or uneducated person who is addicted to drugs or mentally ill, or in a person who has experienced a drastic life event may herald a more severe disease than in patients without these risk indicators, just as the likelihood of a life-threatening infection is higher in an immunocompromised patient than in an otherwise healthy person.*

8.1.4 Be Aware of the Causes of Patient Dissatisfaction with Doctors

The doctor-patient relationship has changed during the last decades. As late as the 1970s, this relationship was characterized by doctors' paternalism. Information given to patients was selected to encourage them to consent to the doctor's decisions. Since then, the paternalistic model has been challenged and replaced by patient-centered medicine that requires the doctor to gain an insight into the patient's ACE, "enter the patient's world and see the illness through the patient's eyes" (Kaba and Sooriakumaran 2007).

Still, as late as the 1990s, the most common patient complaints were the doctor's *rude behavior* (did not respond to my greeting, did not apologize for being late, ignored me, demeaned me, mispronounced my name, and discriminated against me because I am …); *poor patient-doctor communication* (The doctor was in a hurry, did not listen, kept reading my file/looking at the computer monitor, did not understand, made comments that were unrelated to what I told him/her and did not examine my chest even though I said I had difficulty breathing); *poor response to patient's needs for information* (did not explain, I could not understand what he said, ignored my questions; and *poor insight into the patient's state of mind:* (The doctor decided on treatment without consulting me, ignored my concerns, appeared not to believe me, changed the subject when I spoke about my troubles) (Benbassat and Baumal 2001).

Similar complaints were elicited in 2008 from students in an international course for a master's in public health degree at the Hebrew University in Jerusalem (Benbassat unpublished results). The learners were from India, Ghana, El Salvador, Nepal, Kenya, The Philippines, The Palestinian Authority, Nigeria, Liberia, and Haiti. The most common complaint was *poor patient-doctor communication* (The doctor was in a hurry, did not listen, I could not understand his language)(7 of 10 countries); *Rude behavior* (The doctor was in a bad mood, angry, impolite, conceited, especially in public hospitals) (6 of 10 countries); *Failure to meet the patient's needs for information* (Did not explain my complaints and what kind of a disease I have, I could not understand what he said) (6 of 10 countries). Less frequent complaints were doctors' incompetence; failure to examine the patient before prescribing treatment; preferring private patients; and discriminating against poor patients.

Such patient complaints are rarer in the 2020s when patient-centered medicine is the norm in primary clinics (Ha and Longnecker 2010; Agledahl et al. 2011). Not so in hospital emergency wards. A 2002 study concluded that 11% of emergency room patients were dissatisfied mainly because of caregiver conduct and attitudes, specifically with ethnic minorities and patients with poor self-rated health (Goldwag et al. 2002). A 2015 review since 2000 identified gaps between emergency doctors' and patients' perspectives. Patients wanted greater autonomy and complained of poor caregiver attitudes, communication breakdown, and inadequate information, with patients. Average consultation durations in emergency wards were shorter than in primary clinics because of the need for rapid decision-making. Emergency physicians rarely empathized with patients and focused more on patients' physical discomfort and illness, while patients expected psychological comfort and reassurance from physicians and to be treated as individuals (Roh and Park 2016).

8.2 Neglected Guidelines for Teaching

8.2.1 Teach Basic Clinical Skills and Patient Counseling for Mastery

The goal of undergraduate training is to prepare graduates for residency training. However, there seems to be disagreement regarding the learning objectives and teaching content of the undergraduate medical curriculum and the level of competency required of medical school graduates, i.e., what should be taught for general knowledge, mastery, or an intermediate level of competency.

The concept of learning for mastery and its unique features were discussed in Chap. 2. I suggest that medical faculties first, make a clear distinction among the skills that should be taught for mastery, i.e., at a level of proficiency equivalent to that of a practicing physician, and those that are taught at lesser levels of proficiency. Second, teach for mastery of the skills of patient interviewing, physical examination, self-directed learning, and patient counseling.

Today, patient interviewing, physical examination, and self-directed learning are usually taught in preclinical courses and are expected to be reinforced during the clerkship. This approach should be reconsidered for three reasons. First, a low baseline level of required skills may persist. Second, repeated reinforcement throughout the curriculum spreads the responsibility for teaching among many, and individual tutors are not accountable for the outcomes of their teaching. Third, the assumption that students will improve their skills during subsequent practice is inconsistent with the deterioration in physical examination skills with seniority (Mangione and Nieman 1999; Vukanovic-Criley et al. 2006), and with the inverse relationship between the number of years a physician has been in practice and the quality of care he or she provides (Choudhry et al. 2005) that is most likely due to limited updating.

I have repeatedly observed glaring errors in students' examination skills that could be attributed to their tutors. These errors included defining paradoxical breathing, synchronizing the examiner's hand movement with the patient's breathing during palpation of the liver margin, palpation of the thyroid gland, and examination of chest expansion. Some tutors needed to be shown the location of the normal diaphragm during expiration; the absence of cardiac dullness in emphysema; and that limiting the examination of the lungs to the back leaves the upper lobe unexamined. When confronted with such errors, the instructors admitted that they were teaching as they were taught. Therefore, I suggest encouraging students to read the appropriate chapter in the textbooks before their tutor demonstrates a particular skill and discuss with the tutor possible discrepancies between the text and the demonstrated technique.

The most compelling reason for revising the content of the physical examination and for updating its teaching is the availability of hand-held pulse oximeters, spirometry, and point-of-care ultrasound devices (PoCUS). In 2020, my colleagues and I called to update the physical examination by (a) teaching it by clinical contexts, rather than by organ systems, and restricting the traditional head-to-toe physical examination to patients with non-localizing complaints, or symptoms originating from multiple organ systems; (b) restricting the number of maneuvers by discerning between a core of "essential" signs of urgent conditions, "important" signs that should supplement the core as clinically indicated, and "optional" PE signs that are no longer useful (Benbassat and Gilon 2020).

A second topic that I suggest teaching for mastery is the ability to provide counseling on health promotion and disease prevention (HP/DP). "HP/DP" enables individuals to improve their health and prevent illness and injury through access to medical care, health information, and preventive programs. "Patient counseling" consists of the doctor meeting the patient's needs for information about his/her health, providing guidance, and solving problems collaboratively with the patient. *Rather than integrating basic clinical skills and HP/DP as secondary learning objectives throughout the undergraduate curriculum, students would be better served by a single program that aims at imparting the specific aspects of patient interviewing, physical examination, self-directed learning, and providing a patient with counseling on HP/DP at a level of competence that is expected from a practicing physician. Clinical tutors should be held accountable for the results of their teaching.*

8.2.2 Caution Students from Unselective Imitation of Role Models

A role model is a person who is a benchmark of excellence and, in general, role modeling is considered desirable in medical education. However, the original definition of a role model is "a person who occupies the social role to which an individual aspires," and it has been claimed that medical students are attracted to individuals with status (Sinclair 1997). Indeed, during my training in the 1950s and 1960s, I aspired to the prestige of some of my tutors, even though some aspects of their behavior, such as the belief that humiliating trainees would motivate learning, made me feel uncomfortable.

Role modeling is certainly important when it consists of demonstrating skills. However, if one defines it as the learner's unselective imitation of role models, then the benefits of role modeling should be considered along with its harms. I have previously argued that role model imitation may initially help students adapt to the clinical setting. However, if sustained, it can perpetuate undesirable practices, such as disease-centered patient interviewing. I suggested that the value of role modeling can be enhanced by first cautioning students against uncritically imitating role models, and second, encouraging students to reflectively evaluate the behavior of their role models to identify types of behavior worth imitating (Benbassat 2014).

No person always exhibits all the qualities of the ideal clinician. Therefore, students should discern between behaviors rather than tutors. Students' development begins when they realize that their tutor shares their doubts and uncertainties. Therefore, one of the qualities of role models would be openness to express doubts and visibility of reflection.

8.2.3 Make Students Aware of Medical Errors

Until the 1960s, clinical practice had an authoritarian hierarchical structure. It emphasized individual performance, viewed doubt as weakness, and downplayed uncertainty. Medical errors were believed to be rare and due to incompetence. However, as early as 1964, Schimmel reported a startling rate of iatrogenic adverse events; in 1975, Gorowitz and McIntyre claimed that "the physicians' propensity for damaging error is widely denied"; and in 1983, McIntyre and Popper stated that medical students see little evidence of an open admission of medical errors during their clinical training.

Since then, the high prevalence of errors has been repeatedly confirmed (Brennan et al. 1991; Donchin et al. 1995; Assiri et al. 2018). In 1978, Cooper et al. argued that "if the frequency of error is to be decreased, a clearer understanding of the process is needed" and used critical incident analysis to study preventable anesthetic mishaps. The outcomes of their analysis led to the view that avoiding errors requires reporting errors, finding out the causes, rethinking the process, and making the healthcare system as error-resistant as possible by standardizing practice through regulations and algorithms. Since the 1990s, doctors have been required to disclose errors to the involved patients and families. Such disclosure can ease the patients' pain without increasing litigation, and the U.S. Joint Commission has linked this requirement to hospital accreditation (Gallagher et al. 2007).

A prerequisite for reporting errors is a guarantee of impunity for those who commit them, and those who do not report errors they notice must bear some risk. These conditions are unlikely to be met, and a 2003 editorial in the Journal of the American College of Surgeons stated that reporting medical errors is a naïve, costly, and misguided goal (Andrus et al. 2003). Indeed, as recently as the 2020s, reporting errors varied widely across centers, with fear of self-incrimination, punishment, and liability claims being the most cited barriers (Aljabari and Kadhim 2021); and only 4.6% of errors leading to malpractice claims were communicated to the patient at the time of the error (Giraldo et al. 2020).

In 1998, Pilpel et al. (1998) called for educating students about medical errors and proposed a specific teaching program. In 2011, the WHO published its "Patient Safety Curriculum Guide," which identified two main barriers to patient safety education: lack of recognition by educators that it should be part of the curriculum, and reluctance to adopt knowledge, such as ergonomics that originates from outside the profession. The purpose of this section is to review medical error teaching programs since then and draw attention to the importance of including in these programs the doctors' responses to the awareness they committed an error.

8.2.4 Medical Error Teaching Programs

A search of Google Scholar using the key terms "medical error teaching programs" and of the bibliographies of relevant articles yielded a convenience sample of publications aimed first, at raising learners' awareness of the uncertainty of clinical judgment, inevitable fallibility, and the need to reduce the rate of medical errors, and second, at teaching how to respond to medical mistakes by taking responsibility for reporting the error to the administration and communicating it to the patient or family (Benbassat, unpublished data).

The learning objectives of these programs included imparting *knowledge* (e.g., the prevalence of medical errors; human factors in medical errors) through flipped classrooms; *attitudes* (e.g., taking responsibility) through discussions; and *skills* (e.g., teamwork) through simulation exercises with interactive debriefing, problem-based learning, and small group activities (Table 8.1). Most publications dealt with five aspects of medical error. First, human factors in medical errors (Royce et al. 2019; Battles and Shea 2001). Second, proposals for undergraduate (Pilpel et al. 1998; Lester and Tritter 2001) and graduate (Barach 2000; Cosby and Croskerry 2003) teaching programs. Third, the dominant causes of errors (the absence of documentation and transfer of information between staff members; lack of equipment; and absence of adequate labeling (Gopher et al. 1989). Fourth, prevention of

Table 8.1 Objectives of teaching programs for patient safety

Undergraduate (medical students)	Graduate (resident physicians)
Knowledge	
Definition of errors Frequency of medical errors The causes of errors are human factors and work environment, failures of information networks and equipment Uncertainties of clinical practice; clinical reasoning; evidence-based medicine Biases in intuitive judgment Principles of clinical pharmacology Prevalence of hospital-acquired infections and modes of infection transmission	Diagnoses we cannot afford to miss Identification of high-risk patients: Comorbidity, immunological suppression, recent life events, psychiatric disorders, and low socio-economic status Diagnostic and treatment algorithms, practice guidelines, and clinical protocols; risks-benefits judgments Errors in anesthesia, intensive care, and emergency departments
Skills	
Missed diagnoses due to deficient history, and physical examination Teamwork skills, communication, and coordination Plan therapy for common indications and write a safe and legal prescription Recognize and report adverse drug reactions Provide patients with information about their medicines Apply precautions for the prevention of hospital infections Know what to do if exposed to blood or other bodily fluids Allow students to make mistakes in an atmosphere where he or she is not judged but trusted and helped	Encourage suggestions from any team member reporting safety concerns Disclosure of errors to patients and families Complications from invasive procedures and anesthesia Emergencies: Airway management, resuscitation, hypovolemic shock, anaphylaxis, and trauma Preventable iatrogenic cardiac arrest Use of information technology, computerized medication order systems, barcoding systems, medication reconciliation, distinct labeling of medication, and the role of clinical pharmacists in reviewing medication orders Apply principles of asepsis. Use protective clothing and equipment. Be able to discuss hospital-acquired infections with patients and relatives
Attitudes	
Need to acknowledge the error, inform the patient, report, and cope with the error Importance of a culture where errors can be admitted and discussed	Taking responsibility for errors and avoiding the tendency to blame others Importance of reporting of medication errors Necessity to manage errors in a system that is fraught with flaws, and still retain individual responsibility

specific errors, such as in prescribing medications (Weant et al. 2014) and hospital-acquired infections (WHO 2011).

Learners were reported to be satisfied with 7 of 10 undergraduate programs and 7 of 18 graduate and postgraduate programs (Wong et al. 2010). Medical students were interested in discussing the frequency of medical errors and attempts to trace their causes (Pilpel et al. 1998). The fifth aspect was the outcomes of the teaching programs. While most were based on *self-reported* changes in knowledge, attitudes, and skills (Kim et al. 2017), some of them improved patient care: diabetes management, medication lists, childhood immunization rates, and disclosure of medical errors (Wong et al. 2010). Simulations were particularly effective in training to deal with medical errors (Sarfati et al. 2019).

8.2.5 Doctors' Response to the Awareness they Committed an Error

The programs listed in Table 8.1 focus on the main victim of medical errors, the patient, and patient safety is their most important goal. However, it was not until 2000 that Wu coined the term "second victim" to refer to the trauma inflicted on the healthcare providers involved in an error. After a doctor makes a mistake, they experience guilt, loss of confidence, professional dissatisfaction, and burnout. Unlike other stressful professions (e.g., pilots and police officers), healthcare providers are not educated about the stressors following errors and the coping strategies with these stressors (Chung et al. 2018).

As early as 1984, Hilfiker wrote:

> ...since doctors do not discuss their mistakes, they do not know how other physicians cope with them. The drastic consequences of errors, the repeated opportunity to make them, the uncertainty of culpability, and the professional denial that mistakes happen, ... create an intolerable dilemma for the physician... We see the horror of our mistakes, yet we cannot deal with their enormous emotional impact.

Four years later Mizrahi (1984) drew attention to the maladaptive mechanisms used by medical residents in coping with their errors. These included *denial* (negation of the concept of error; forgetting the mistakes); *discounting* (blaming the system, superiors, or subordinates); and *distancing* ("no one is perfect"). However, notwithstanding these mechanisms "profound doubts and guilt remained …. [as well as] questions of culpability and responsibility" (Mizrahi 1984). Indeed, physicians respond to their errors with guilt, fear of more errors, loss of confidence, vulnerability, reduced job satisfaction, weakened reputation, and burnout (Tawfik et al. 2018).

These feelings are especially strong within 1 year after graduation (Tyssen and Vaglum 2002; Engel et al. 2006). They can be reduced by emotional support, admitting the mistake to the patient, acknowledging the inevitability of mistakes, and focusing on what changes can be made at the individual and institutional level to prevent recurrence (Wu 2000; Seys et al. 2013). Similarly, a 2020 meta-analysis sorted doctors' coping strategies into task-oriented (following guidelines more closely; better monitoring of the patient; disclosing the error to the patient) and emotion-oriented (disclosing the error; seeking support) (Busch et al. 2020). Yet reviews have identified also dysfunctional coping mechanisms that included keeping feelings to oneself; having fantasies of how things might turn out (Seys et al.

2013); trusting others less; distancing; trying to hide errors; avoiding patients, and procedures; drinking or using drugs (Busch et al. 2020).

There have been two calls for such educational programs. In 2015, Daniels (2015) proposed imparting to nurse anesthetists knowledge on the second victim syndrome, its consequences, coping, and support systems. In 2017, the Resident Wellness Summit proposed a four-modules program. Each consisted of a reading assignment that established a knowledge base and encouraged reflection before classroom group discussions. The first module dealt with the concept of the second victim syndrome. The next one taught how to recognize it in colleagues, and to perform a debriefing after a significant mistake. The third module made learners aware of available resources at their institution. The fourth module focused on the prevention of the second victim syndrome through changes in the prevailing culture (Chung et al. 2018).

I concur with the suggestions to include programs on the second victim syndrome in the curriculum. After participating in these programs, students may seek counseling in an atmosphere where they are not judged as they are in admissions interviews, but supported as they consider their future careers.

8.2.6 Professional Distress

A major source of professional distress, unrelated to practice characteristics and personality traits, arises when interns and residents grasp that the realities of clinical practice differ from what they expected. In 2011, my colleagues and I suggested informing students about the types and frequency of professional distress, with a view of creating realistic expectations and making students realize that professional distress is pervasive rather than due to individual inadequacies (Benbassat et al. 2011). After participating in teaching modules such as those described by Chung et al. (2018), students may wish to receive counseling, in an atmosphere in which they are not judged but rather assisted in considering future careers. A student, whose incentive to study medicine is a need to be trusted, may wish to consider the frequency of patient litigation against doctors. Students whose main motivation is a need to be in control may be concerned by the limitations in doctors' autonomy. Patients with psychosocial problems may frustrate students with a bio-medical orientation. Finally, students who feel intolerant of uncertainty may wish to choose a non-clinical career.

8.2.7 Inconsistencies Between Theory and Practice

Physicians' life satisfaction is lowest, and the prevalence of psychological problems is highest within 1 year of graduation (Tyssen and Vaglum 2002). No less than 76% of U.S. residents exhibited high levels of burnout (Shanafelt et al. 2002), and 22%

of Canadian residents reported that they would not choose medicine if allowed to relive their careers (Cohen and Patten 2005).

It seems that when confronted with the reality of clinical practice, medical graduates find it different than they expected. One such discrepancy is between the pervasive uncertainties in clinical practice and their denial in the educational setting (Gerrity et al. 1992), which may lead some graduates to attribute their doubts to personal inadequacies. There is also a discrepancy between the biomedical orientation of medical training and the high proportion of patients with psychosocial problems. The transition from a physician trained to "fix" problems to a therapist whose job is to "be there" can be stressful (Krebs et al. 2006). Another training-practice gap is the expectation to provide state-of-the-art care and physicians' failure to keep updated. It has been reported that physicians' clinical competence decreases with increasing years in practice (Choudhry et al. 2005), and physicians' awareness of not being up to date may increase their feelings of guilt and fear of making mistakes (Kushnir et al. 2000).

Medical students should be informed that the stress they may experience in the first few years after graduation is pervasive and that discrepancies between training and practice should not lead to feelings of personal inadequacy but should be further explored and reduced through changes in clinical training. Some medical schools have already made some of these changes. There are calls to change the culture of clinical teaching to make physicians' uncertainties visible (Djulbegovic 2004). Evidence-based practice not only acknowledges uncertainty; it attempts to quantify it by distinguishing between different levels of evidence. *Setting realistic expectations for medical students can reduce future stress.*

References

Agledahl KM, Gulbrandsen P, Førde R, Wifstad Å. Courteous but not curious: how doctors' politeness masks their existential neglect. A qualitative study of video-recorded patient consultations. J Med Ethics. 2011;37(11):650–4.
Aljabari S, Kadhim Z. Common barriers to reporting medical errors. Sci World J. 2021;10:2021.
Andrus CH, Villasenor EG, Kettelle JB, Roth R, Sweeney AM, Matolo NM. "To err is human": uniformly reporting medical errors and near misses, a naïve, costly, and misdirected goal. J Am Coll Surg. 2003;196:911–8.
Antonovsky A. Social class, life expectancy, and overall mortality. Milbank Mem Q. 1967;45:31–73.
Assiri GA, Shebl NA, Mahmoud MA, Aloudah N, Grant E, Aljadhey H, Sheikh A. What is the epidemiology of medication errors, error-related adverse events, and risk factors for errors in adults managed in community care contexts? A systematic review of international literature. BMJ Open. 2018;8:e019101.
Barach P. Patient safety curriculum. Acad Med. 2000;75:551–2.
Battles JB, Shea CE. A system of analyzing medical errors to improve GME curricula and programs. Acad Med. 2001;76:125–33.
Benbassat J. Role modeling in medical education: the importance of a reflective imitation. Acad Med. 2014;89(4):550–4.

Benbassat J, Baumal R. Teaching doctor-patient interviewing skills using an integrated learner and teacher-centered approach. Am J Med Sci. 2001;322:349–57.

Benbassat J, Gilon D. Teaching the physical examination by context and by integrating hand-held ultrasound devices. Med Teach. 2020;42:993–9.

Benbassat J, Baumal R, Chan S, Nirel N. Sources of distress during medical training and clinical practice: suggestions for reducing their impact. Med Teach. 2011;33:486–90.

Brennan TA, Leape LL, Laird NM, Hebert L, Localio AR, Lawthers AG, Newhouse JP, Weiler PC, Hiatt HH. Incidence of adverse events and negligence in hospitalized patients: results of the Harvard medical practice study I. N Engl J Med. 1991;324:370–6.

Busch IM, Moretti F, Purgato M, Barbui C, Wu AW, Rimondini M. Dealing with adverse events: a meta-analysis on second victims' coping strategies. J Patient Saf. 2020;16:e51–60.

Choudhry NK, Fletcher RH, Soumerai SB. Systematic review: the relationship between clinical experience and quality of health care. Ann Intern Med. 2005;142:260–73.

Chung AS, Smart J, Zdradzinski M, Roth S, Gende A, Conroy K, Battaglioli N. Educator toolkits on second victim syndrome, mindfulness and meditation, and positive psychology: the 2017 resident wellness consensus summit. Western J Emerg Med. 2018;19:327.

Cohen JS, Patten S. Well-being in residency training: a survey examining resident physician satisfaction both within and outside of residency training and mental health in Alberta. BMC Med Educ. 2005;5:1–1.

Cooper JB, Newbower RS, Long CD, McPeek B. Preventable anesthesia mishaps: a study of human factors. Anesthesiology. 1978;49:399–406.

Cosby KS, Croskerry P. Patient safety: a curriculum for teaching patient safety in emergency medicine. Acad Emerg Med. 2003;10:69–78.

Daniels R "Design Of An Evidence-Based Second Victim Curriculum For Nurse Anesthetists". 2015. Yale School of Nursing Digital Theses. 1028. https://elischolar.library.yale.edu/ysndt/1028. Accessed Apr 2024.

Djulbegovic B. Lifting the fog of uncertainty from the practice of medicine. BMJ. 2004;329:1419–20.

Donchin Y, Gopher D, Olin M, Badihi Y, Biesky MR, Sprung CL, Pizov R, Cotev S. A look into the nature and causes of human errors in the intensive care unit. Crit Care Med. 1995;23:294–300.

Engel KG, Rosenthal M, Sutcliffe KM. Residents' responses to medical error: coping, learning, and change. Acad Med. 2006;81:86–93.

Gallagher TH, Studdert D, Levinson W. Disclosing harmful medical errors to patients. N Engl J Med. 2007;356:2713–9.

Gerrity MS, Earp JAL, DeVellis RF, Light DW. Uncertainty and professional work: Perception of physicians in clinical practice. Amer J Sociol. 1992;97:1022–51.

Giraldo P, Sato L, Castells X. The impact of incident disclosure behaviors on medical malpractice claims. J Patient Saf. 2020;16:e225–9.

Glei DA, Preston SH. Estimating the impact of drug use on US mortality, 1999–2016. PLoS One. 2020;15:e0226732.

Goldman RE, Sullivan A, Back AL, Alexander SC, Matsuyama RK, Lee SJ. Patients' reflections on communication in the second-opinion hematology-oncology consultation. Patient Educ Couns. 2009;76:44–50.

Goldwag R, Berg A, Yuval D, Benbassat J. Predictors of patient dissatisfaction with emergency care. IMAJ. 2002;4(8):603–6.

Gopher D, Olin M, Badihi Y, Cohen G, Donchin Y, Bieski M, Cotev S. The nature and causes of human errors in a medical intensive care unit. In: Proceedings of the human factors society annual meeting, vol. 33. Los Angeles: SAGE; 1989, October. p. 956–60.

Gorovitz S, MacIntyre A. Toward a theory of medical fallibility. Hastings Cent Rep. 1975;5:13–23.

Ha JF, Longnecker N. Doctor-patient communication: a review. Ochsner J. 2010;10(1):38–43.

Hilfiker D. Facing our mistakes. N Engl J Med. 1984;310:118–22.

Hillen MA, Medendorp NM, Daams JG, Smets EMA. Patient-driven second opinions in oncology: a systematic review. Oncologist. 2017;22:1197–211.

Holmes TH, Rahe RH. The social readjustment rating scale. J Psychosom Res. 1967;11:213–8.

Kaba R, Sooriakumaran P. The evolution of the doctor-patient relationship. Int J Surg. 2007;5(1):57–65.

Kark JD, Goldman S, Epstein L. Iraqi missile attacks on Israel: the association of mortality with a life-threatening stressor. JAMA. 1995;273(15):1208–10.

Kim CW, Myung SJ, Eo EK, Chang Y. Improving disclosure of medical error through educational program as a first step toward patient safety. BMC Med Educ. 2017;17:1–6.

Krebs EE, Garrett JM, Konrad TR. The difficult doctor? Characteristics of physicians who report frustration with patients: An analysis of survey data. BMC Health Serv Res. 2006;6:128.

Kushnir T, Cohen AH, Kitai E. Continuing medical education and primary physicians' job stress, burnout and dissatisfaction. Med Educ. 2000;34:430–43.

Lee SA, Nam CM, Kim YH, Kim TH, Jang SI, Park EC. Impact of onset of psychiatric disorders and psychiatric treatment on mortality among patients with cancer. Oncologist. 2020;25:e733–42.

Lester H, Tritter JQ. Medical error: a discussion of the medical construction of error and suggestions for reforms of medical education to decrease error. Med Educ. 2001;35:855–61.

Mangione S, Nieman LZ. Pulmonary auscultatory skills during training in internal medicine and family practice. Am J Respir Crit Care Med. 1999;159:1119–24.

McIntyre N, Popper K. The critical attitude in medicine: the need for a new ethics. Br Med J (Clin Res Ed). 1983;287:1919.

Mizrahi T. Managing medical mistakes: ideology, insularity and accountability among internists-in-training. Soc Sci Med. 1984;19:135–46.

Noone PA. The Holmes–Rahe stress inventory. Occup Med. 2017;67:581–2.

Ospina NS, Phillips KA, Rodriguez-Gutierrez R, Castaneda-Guarderas A, Gionfriddo MR, Branda ME, Montori VM. Eliciting the patient's agenda-secondary analysis of recorded clinical encounters. J Gen Intern Med. 2019;34:36–40.

Pilpel D, Schor R, Benbassat J. Barriers to acceptance of medical error: the case for a teaching program. Med Educ. 1998;32:3–7.

Rico-Uribe LA, Caballero FF, Martín-María N, Cabello M, Ayuso-Mateos JL, Miret M. Association of loneliness with all-cause mortality: a meta-analysis. PLoS One. 2018;13:e0190033.

Rodgers J, Cuevas AG, Williams DR, Kawachi I, Subramanian SV. The relative contributions of behavioral, biological, and psychological risk factors in the association between psychosocial stress and all-cause mortality among middle-and older-aged adults in the USA. GeroScience. 2021;43:655–72.

Roh H, Park KH. A scoping review: communication between emergency physicians and patients in the emergency department. J Emerg Med. 2016;50(5):734–43.

Royce CS, Hayes MM, Schwartzstein RM. Teaching critical thinking: a case for instruction in cognitive biases to reduce diagnostic errors and improve patient safety. Acad Med. 2019;94:187–94.

Ruetters D, Keinki C, Schroth S, Liebl P, Huebner J. Is there evidence for a better health care for cancer patients after a second opinion? A systematic review. J Cancer Res Clin Oncol. 2016;142:1521–8.

Sarfati L, Ranchon F, Vantard N, Schwiertz V, Larbre V, Parat S, Faudel A, Rioufol C. Human-simulation-based learning to prevent medication error: a systematic review. J Eval Clin Pract. 2019;25:11–20.

Schimmel EM. The hazards of hospitalization. Ann Intern Med. 1964;60:100–10.

Seys D, Wu AW, Gerven EV, Vleugels A, Euwema M, Panella M, Scott SD, Conway J, Sermeus W, Vanhaecht K. Health care professionals as second victims after adverse events: a systematic review. Eval Health Prof. 2013;36:135–62.

Shanafelt TD, Bradley KA, Wipf JE, Back AL. Burnout and self-reported patient care in an internal medicine residency program. Ann Intern Med. 2002;136:358–67.

References

Sinclair S. Making doctors: an institutional apprenticeship. Oxford: Berg; 1997. As quoted by: Paice E, Heard S, Moss F. How important are role models in making good doctors? BMJ, 2002; 325: 707–10.

Stringhini S, Carmeli C, Jokela M, Avendaño M, Muennig P, Guida F, Ricceri F, d'Errico A, Barros H, Bochud M, Chadeau-Hyam M. Socioeconomic status and the 25× 25 risk factors as determinants of premature mortality: a multicohort study and meta-analysis of 1·7 million men and women. Lancet. 2017;389:1229–37.

Suchman AL, Markakis K, Beckman HB, Frankel R. A model of empathic communication in the medical interview. JAMA. 1997;277:678–82.

Tawfik DS, Profit J, Morgenthaler TI, Satele DV, Sinsky CA, Dyrbye LN, Tutty MA, West CP, Shanafelt TD. Physician burnout, well-being, and work unit safety grades in relationship to reported medical errors. Mayo Clin Proc. 2018;93(11):1571–80.

Tosteson ANA, Yang Q, Nelson HD, Longton G, Soneji SS, Pepe M, Geller B, Carney PA, Onega T, Allison KH, Elmore JG, Weaver DL. Second opinion strategies in breast pathology: a decision analysis addressing over-treatment, under-treatment, and care costs. Breast Cancer Res Treat. 2018;167:195–203.

Tyssen R, Vaglum P. Mental health problems among young physicians: an updated review of prospective studies. Harv Rev Psychiatry. 2002;10:154–65.

Vukanovic-Criley JM, Criley S, Warde CM, Boker JR, Guevara-Matheus L, Churchill WH, Nelson WP, Criley JM. Competency in cardiac examination skills in medical students, trainees, physicians, and faculty. Arch Intern Med. 2006;166:610–6.

Weant KA, Bailey AM, Baker SN. Strategies for reducing medication errors in the emergency department. Open Access Emerg Med. 2014;6:45–55.

WHO. Patient safety curriculum guide: multi-professional edition. Geneva: WHO; 2011. WHO patient safety curriculum guide.pdf. Accessed June 2023.

Williams DR, Mohammed SA. Discrimination and racial health disparities: evidence and needed research. J Behav Med. 2009;32:20–47.

Wong BM, Etchells EE, Kuper A, Levinson W, Shojania KG. Teaching quality improvement and patient safety to trainees: a systematic review. Acad Med. 2010;85:1425–39.

Wu AW. Medical error: the second victim. The doctor who makes the mistake needs help too. BMJ. 2000;320:726–7.

Chapter 9
Issues that May Require Curricular Changes

Abstract Experts agree that there is a gap between how physicians are trained and the needs of the healthcare system. Already today, the traditional focus on knowledge is being expanded to include competence and the ability to deal with unfamiliar clinical problems. Undergraduate medical curricula are redesigned to include decision theory, information access, and critical interpretation of evidence. Realizing that hospitals no longer provide an appropriate learning environment has led to allocating clinical clerkships to primary, consultant, and perinatal outpatient clinics.

This section addresses topics that may require additional curricular changes. Medical schools may wish to reconsider their selection of applicants, attempt to shorten the duration of medical education, and promote student well-being. Second, they should develop methods to teach students social and behavioral sciences, clinical reasoning, effective teamwork and avoidance of unprofessional behavior, and how to handle time-limited doctor-patient encounters. Third, review the appropriateness of the clinical learning environment in hospitals that allow private treatment in countries with universal health insurance. Finally, consider combining the final evaluation of medical school graduates with counseling regarding their future careers.

9.1 Selection of Applicants for Undergraduate Medical Training[1]

9.1.1 The Problem

The task of medical school admissions committees is to select a limited number of students from a large pool of seemingly suitable applicants. The selection is expected to be fair, based on merit, evidence-based, and legally defensible, as well as to state the medical school's mission and contribute to diversity among trainees (Marrin et al. 2004). Medical schools differ in their interpretation of fairness and merit (Admissions to Higher Education Steering Group 2007) and appear to be guided by one of the following premises.

The first is that the competence of medical school graduates depends on the quality of the teaching program at their school, and the applicants' attributes on admission are of little predictive value. Therefore, medical students are selected by a lottery among eligible applicants. The second interprets merit as past cognitive (academic) achievements and admission is offered to applicants with the highest point averages (GPAs) or A levels in the UK, and aptitude tests. GPAs assess knowledge of subjects, such as chemistry and mathematics. Aptitude tests assess reasoning, intelligence, and culturally acquired knowledge, such as vocabulary and geography. GPAs and aptitude tests are reliable, i.e., reproducible when applied to the same individual and they predict success on examinations in medical school (Eveland et al. 2022), scores on licensing examinations (Kulatunga Moruzi and Norman 2002; Julian 2005), internship ratings (Ferguson et al. 2002) and career progression (McManus et al. 2003). The scores obtained on the Medical College Admission Test (MCAT) have been reported to predict the performance on the USMLE part I (Donnon et al. 2007) and the Canadian Licensing Examinations—part II (communication and problem exploration skills) (Kulatunga Moruzi and Norman 2002), and regression analyses have indicated that the GPA and the MCAT scores have an independent predictive validity for medical school grades and USMLE scores (Julian 2005).

The third premise defines merit as qualities beyond cognitive achievements. These "noncognitive" traits include a capacity for independent learning, interpersonal communication, empathy, teamwork, and the "attributes of a stable adult" (Albanese et al. 2003). During the past decades, there has been a shift in favor of this third premise. In the 1970s, the medical schools of Newcastle in Australia (Feletti et al. 1985), McMaster in Ontario (Kulatunga Moruzi and Norman 2002), and Beer-Sheva in Israel (Antonovsky 1987) adopted admission policies aimed at

---

[1] Previous versions of this sub-section were published in Benbassat J, Baumal R. Uncertainties in the selection of applicants for medical school. Advances in Health Sciences Education. 2007; 12: 509–21. Benbassat J. Assessments of non-academic attributes in applicants for undergraduate medical education: an overview of advantages and limitations. Medical Science Educator. 2019; 29: 1129–34. With permissions through the Copyright Clearance Center.

identifying applicants who possessed desirable non-cognitive traits, in addition to academic achievements. Since 1997, other medical schools in Australia have adopted similar admission policies (Turnbull et al. 2003). A 2006 survey of 22 UK medical schools found that, but for two, they all used some non-cognitive criteria for admission (Parry et al. 2006). In 2001, even Holland abandoned its traditional lottery-based admissions policy and adopted one considering the applicant's non-academic attributes. The quest for non-cognitive attributes is a costly endeavor. How justified is it?

9.1.2 Non-cognitive Attributes: Advantages and Limitations

Assessment of non-academic attributes carries three benefits. First, it complies with the medical school accreditation requirement in North America, which states that admission policies include assessments of non-academic attributes to ensure that applicants possess the personal and emotional characteristics necessary for them to become competent physicians (Functions and Structure of a Medical School 2016). Second, it responds to societal demands (ten Cate 2007). Third, it attests to the mission and values of the medical school (Marrin et al. 2004).

As recently as 2008, non-cognitive attributes were mostly inferred from interviewing the applicants (Monroe et al. 2013). However, a 2016 literature review found that interviews lack the reliability and validity required for high-stakes screening (Patterson et al. 2016a). Another systematic review compared the characteristics and outcomes of medical students admitted with and without unstructured and semi-structured interviews. It found that the cohorts had similar academic and clinical performance and mental health issues. Structured interviews admitted students who scored higher on clinical and social competence and lower on academic exams by their final year of medical school (Lin et al. 2024).

Consequently, to inform admission decisions, medical schools increasingly use selection centers (SCs) that employ one or more of the following: multiple-choice question testing, interviews, writing essays, listening to a lecture, and answering questions about its content (O'Neill et al. 2009), situational judgment tests (SJTs) (Patterson et al. 2017), small group discussions of a problem (Collins et al. 1995), multiple mini-interviews (MMI) (Eva et al. 2004), simulated tutorials (Kulatunga Moruzi and Norman 2002), and studying a text and explaining it to another candidate (ten Cate and Smal 2002), as well as the applicants' demographic data, their scores on personality tests, their statements/essays/autobiographical letters and letters of recommendation.

MMIs are rotations among 10–12 stations, at which applicants discuss health-related issues with an examiner or interact with a standardized person while observed by an examiner. SJTs consist of written or videotaped situations that applicants may encounter (De Leng et al. 2017). Tests of personality traits usually focus on conscientiousness (responsibility, self-discipline) (Haight et al. 2012; McLarnon et al. 2017), emotional intelligence (monitoring one's own and other's emotions)

(Cook et al. 2016), and empathy (understanding and responding to another person's concerns) (Hojat et al. 2013). The reliability, i.e., internal consistency (Cronbach alpha) of personality tests has been reported to be 0.81 (Hamby et al. 2016) and of SJTs 0.43–0.94 (Patterson et al. 2016b). SCs have an alpha of 0.88–0.91; inter-rater correlations of 0.62–0.77; test-retest correlations of 0.59–0.43; and G coefficient of 0.82 (O'Neill et al. 2009; Gafni et al. 2012). MMIs have an alpha of 0.61–0.98; inter-rater correlations of 0.41–0.91; test-retest correlations of 0.34–0.72; and generalizability over other settings (G coefficient) of 0.51–0.88 (Jerant et al. 2017).

These assessments have several limitations. First, non-academic skills are difficult to identify and measure. For example, empathy is defined as a cognitive understanding of another person's perspective or an affective response to another person's plight; it has been variably measured by peer ratings, patient ratings, pencil-and-paper tests, and various rating scales of an observed behavior (Benbassat and Baumal 2004). Disagreement exists regarding the definition of emotional intelligence (personality trait? learnable attribute?), with different definitions leading to different instruments for its assessment (Carrothers et al. 2000).

Second, there are about 80 such attributes in the categories of ethical responsibility, dependability, service orientation, social skills, capacity for improvement, resilience and adaptability, cultural competence, communication, and teamwork (Koenig et al. 2013); no admission process can consider all of them, and focusing only on some of them cannot be logically justified. Third, it is uncertain what each of the presently used tests of nonacademic attributes assesses. It has been claimed that "tests like the MMI are less tests of a specific characteristic and more a test format adaptable to assessing many different attributes [which] regrettably leaves the specific attribute in the eye of the beholder—the author of the specific test" (Hecker and Norman 2017).

Fourth, even assuming that desirable non-academic attributes can be identified on admission, it is uncertain whether these attributes are permanent across lifespans and contexts (Ferguson and Lievens 2017). Fifth, even if they are permanent, the commonly used outcomes in validation studies (dropout rates, scores on professionalism, scores on communication skills, peer and clinical instructors' ratings) may not attest to clinical competence (Patterson et al. 2017b).

Sixth, even if they attest to clinical competence, the reported correlations are low to moderate (Niessen and Meijer 2016). Reported correlations between MMIs on admission and peer assessments during the clerkships were 0.39 (Hadad et al. 2016); between SJT and supervisor assessments were 0.34 (Patterson et al. 2017); and between scores on selection centers and OSCE scores 4 years later were 0.41 (Rotthoff et al. 2014). Reported coefficients of correlations between personality tests and success on examinations ranged between 0.22 and 0.32 (Ferguson et al. 2002), and between scores on psychosocial questionnaires, and basic sciences grades, clinical sciences grades, and clinical clerkships ratings between 0.37 and 0.41 (Hojat et al. 1993). More recent studies reported that the correlation between conscientiousness on admission and clerkship performance was 0.15 (McLarnon et al. 2017).

These correlations predict less than 10–20% of the variance in outcomes and successful applicants who lack the attribute under consideration may outnumber those who possess it. Their uncertain predictive value is also due to the unknown prevalence of the desirable non-cognitive traits in the applicants' pool (the "pretest" or "prior" probability) of the non-cognitive trait under consideration. For example, an 80% sensitive and 80% specific test for "empathy" would increase (if positive) the prevalence of empathy from 1% to 4%, or from 50% to 80%, and would decrease (if negative) this prevalence from 1% to 0.2%, or from 50% to 20%. In other words, using non-cognitive admission criteria would inevitably lead to the rejection of applicants who possess the desirable non-cognitive trait under consideration and in the admission of applicants who lack this trait. Certainly, no practicing physician would employ diagnostic tests with validities similar to those of the non-cognitive criteria for admissions to medical schools, to diagnose diseases with unknown pretest probabilities.

Seventh, even if the magnitude of correlations were high, medical faculties are only rarely aware of the possible "dark side" of "good" traits (Ferguson and Lievens 2017). There is evidence that conscientiousness is inversely correlated with creativity (Patterson and Zibarras 2017). There is also conflicting evidence on the associations of desirable personality traits with well-being. Excessive empathy has been linked to guilt feelings and depression, and empathic tendencies have been claimed to be "risky strengths" (Tone and Tully 2014).

Furthermore, it is uncertain whether the use of non-academic attributes in the selection process is morally defensible (Norman 2004). It stands to reason that applicants who are rejected because of insufficient academic achievements would understand the reason for their failure. However, rejection after "failing" tests for nonacademic attributes may affect one's self-esteem, particularly in the absence of feedback. I feel uncomfortable that my profession guided by the principle "do no harm," does not consider the possible harm of employing admission processes that purport to select virtuous applicants. Ninth, even assuming that such a selection was morally defensible, it is uncertain whether it is legally defensible. Despite the pervasive esteem of doctors' desirable non-academic attributes, it is uncertain whether society would accept the absence of such attributes as a reason for denying the opportunity to become a doctor, mainly because of the next and most compelling argument against using them to inform medical school admissions: *society needs not only practicing doctors but also those in specialties such as research, administration, preventive medicine, public health, and diagnostic medicine. Different careers require different attributes.* For example, compassion is important for people-oriented, but less for technology-oriented specialties.

9.1.3 Competing Values

A survey of Canadian medical faculty, medical students, and people in the community revealed that fairness and validity were the most valued qualities of the admission process for medical schools (Marrin et al. 2004). An example of incompatibility between these values is whether a medical school should adopt a race-conscious affirmative action admission policy. A selection based solely on cognitive criteria provides a fair admission process. A race-conscious preference gives a special advantage to ethnic minorities who are more likely to practice in underserved populations (Hull et al. 1996; Rabinowitz 1993; Hsueh et al. 2004) and fosters a multicultural medical school environment. In the specific case of race-conscious affirmative action, the Supreme Court has ruled that it is constitutional in the USA (Lakhan 2003). However, in addition to affirmative action, medical school admission committees often face other dilemmas, such as whether to admit brilliant applicants with severe handicaps.

9.1.4 Conclusions

Two conclusions emerge from this unsystematic review. First, the use of non-cognitive admission criteria is not evidence-based. This should not preclude prospective, longitudinal studies of their validity. There is some evidence that the MMI (Eva et al. 2004) and Goldberg's ("big 5") adjectives (Ferguson et al. 2003) do predict future performance on clinical skills and basic science grades, respectively. Similarly, the predictive value of the performance of specific assignments (ten Cate and Smal 2002; Collins et al. 1995; Eva et al. 2004) and the applicants' moral orientation (Bore et al. 2005) and moral reasoning (Benor et al. 1984) should be explored further. The optimal number of repeat admission interviews that would achieve acceptable levels of reliability should be determined. There is evidence that the combined predictive validity of admission criteria, such as GPA, aptitude tests, personal statements, and personality tests is higher than that of each of these criteria alone (Ferguson et al. 2003). Therefore, further research may attempt to identify criteria with additive predictive value using multivariate analyses. Finally, the predictive validity of the applicants' biographical data (Oswald et al. 2004) for the various outcome measures should be determined. All these studies should be performed for research, rather than for decision-making about admissions.

Second, the main "filter" that defines who will enter medical school, is not the admission process, but rather an individual's decision to apply for admission. Consequently, I concur with the Higher Education Steering Group in the UK, which has called for an admission system that "... provides the information that applicants need to make an informed choice. This should include the institution's admission policy, detailed criteria for admission, and an explanation of the admission process. It should [also] include a general indication of the weight given to prior academic achievements and potential demonstrated by other means" (Admissions to Higher Education Steering Group 2007, p. 7). Others have similarly suggested that medical schools must make explicit the criteria for admission in bulletins distributed to applicants (Nowacek and Sachs 1990). Such information should include the most common causes of dissatisfaction and burnout among practicing clinicians; the prevalence of medical errors and litigation for medical negligence; and the prevalence of patient violence against physicians. This information may help applicants make an informed decision based on a realistic self-appraisal.

It may be argued that the self-selection of applicants for medical school may be flawed by a tendency to an exaggerated self-evaluation since they are not mature enough to assess their abilities, motives, and future aims realistically. It may also be claimed that decisions to apply to medical schools are often motivated by irrelevant factors, such as parental influence, anticipated income, and prestige. However, I believe that, by providing information on the strains of a life in medicine, admission committees will reduce the applicants' tendencies to exaggerated self-assessments, mitigate possible misguided motives, and lead to more rational decisions regarding whether to apply to medical school. Providing such information does not aim at reducing the number of applicants, but rather to improve the composition of the applicants' pool.

Two prospective studies are unique in addressing some of these difficulties. One sought a correlation between the performance of UK students on academic and non-academic psychometric tests on admission, and the outcome variables of academic performance, professional behavior, clinical competence, and communication skills on follow-up (Adam et al. 2015). The second study compared the outcomes of four groups of Dutch medical students: those offered immediate admission because of top past academic achievements; those admitted after participating in a voluntary SC; those who had been rejected by the voluntary SC but accepted by lottery; and those admitted by lottery without participating in the SC (Wouters et al. 2017).

A consistent finding of both studies was that students with top past academic achievements outperformed other students, not only during the first 3 years in medical school but also during the clerkship rotations. The authors concluded that "... prior academic performance was the only item used in the selection procedure that was a useful, significant predictor of progress" (Adam et al. 2015) and "a selection [for non-academic attributes], which is usually costly, seems to be of little additional value compared to a weighted lottery procedure" (Wouters et al. 2017). Still, an ever-increasing number of medical schools use various assessments of non-academic attributes to inform admissions, despite the cost, lack of evidence, and questionable morality of such evaluations. Meeting societal expectations outweighs considerations of validity and cost.

How then can medical education promote non-academic attributes that, beyond their contribution to professional competence, are essential for the welfare of society? Like Niessen and Meijer (2016), I suggest doing this by indoctrination, assessments, and counseling during medical training. Already today, many non-academic attributes are subject to formal indoctrination and role modeling. Hopefully, in the future, clinical preceptors will also assume the responsibility for discussing the professional lapses of students and faculty in an atmosphere characterized by respect and critical reflection. Already today, clinical preceptors evaluate students' non-academic attributes during the clerkship rotations.

I propose supplementing these assessments by implementing MMIs, SJTs, and personality tests during the final year in medical school. Certainly, this would be less expensive than their implementation on the entire body of medical school applicants. These assessments would serve as a point of departure for individual feedback on students' performance during the rotation and counseling regarding students' possible strengths and weaknesses for specific specialties. Providers of feedback and counseling would emphasize with due humility the limitations of MMIs, SJTs, SCs, and personality tests, address the "dark sides" of conscientiousness, empathy, and emotional intelligence, and attempt to identify the optimal degree of these traits that predict both competence and well-being.

Therefore, I believe that the quest for "non-academic" qualifications in screening medical school candidates will be the subject of critical review and may even be canceled. The selection of medical students may be based either on past academic achievements, a lottery, or various combinations thereof.

9.2 Personalizing Medical Education and Reducing its Duration[2]

A major weakness of the medical curriculum is its duration. In both North America and Europe, it lasts for about 7 years. Yet, medical school graduates cannot provide unsupervised patient care unless they have completed an additional residency of up to 7 years. Furthermore, the medical curriculum does not meet the demand for medical manpower. There has been a shortage of GPs since the 1950s (Brotherton et al. 2001) and more recently, in other specialties (Lupu 2010). Finally, the content of the training is based on three false assumptions.

The first misconception is that it is relevant to all medical specialties. It is not. The current undergraduate medical curriculum is inconsistent with the career requirements of many of its graduates. It has already been pointed out that "the job characteristics of a neurosurgeon, a public health physician, a pathologist, and a psychiatrist are almost as different as those of a physician, a pilot, an accountant, or a museum curator" (McManus et al. 2006). Indeed, human anatomy is relevant to radiologists but not to epidemiologists and the behavioral sciences are germane to primary care physicians but not to pathologists.

Second, students' exposure mostly to inpatients assumes that clinical problem-solving is a general ability that, once acquired, can be applied to patients in any

---

[2] A previous version of this section was published in Benbassat J, Baumal R. Expected benefits of streamlining undergraduate medical education by early commitment to specific medical specialties. Advances in health sciences education. 2012 Mar; 17:145–55. With permission through the Copyright Clearance Center.

setting. However, this assumption is at odds with evidence that competence is subject-specific rather than general and with the agreement that problem-solving and sound decision-making depend more on context-bound expertise in a specialty than on general strategies (Perkins and Salomon 1989).

Third, undergraduate medical education assumes that all specialties share the same code of professional ethics. This is incorrect: clinicians are committed to individual patients, public health specialists to populations, and researchers to the promotion of science. The fourth assumption is that some personality traits, such as empathy, are equally important for all medical specialties, and, therefore, medical school admissions should attempt to identify applicants who appear to have these traits. This assumption is similarly incorrect: not all medical school graduates choose a clinical career.

These problems have led to proposed individualized undergraduate programs aimed at training for different medical specialties. These proposals are not novel. Separate undergraduate training paths exist already today for medically aligned professions, such as dentistry and nursing and it has been argued that "specialties ..., such as ophthalmology and cardiology, lend themselves to a radically different educational approach, such as complete six-year courses commencing from matriculation" (van Niekerk 2009). The main limitation of these proposals is that they depart radically from the 300-year tradition of medical education and are not likely to be implemented by medical educators alone.

It may be argued that high school graduates are too immature and poorly informed to commit to a specific medical specialty. Yet, already at present, high school graduates are committing themselves to nursing and dentistry, and, after graduating, most of them pursue the careers to which they committed themselves. Furthermore, it has been reported that 45% of the students predicted their ultimate specialty choice already at entry to medical school, thereby indicating that "specialty choices are made early and are more stable and accurate than the previous literature has suggested" (Zeldow et al. 1992). Therefore, I believe that an effort to inform applicants for medical training about the various medical specialties will help medical school applicants commit themselves to specific careers.

To address these problems, it has been suggested to replace the medical curricula with shorter courses of study focused on training for different medical professions similar to those for dentistry and nursing (Benbassat and Baumal 2012) that would prepare for residency training in secondary and tertiary specialties; residency training in primary care (family medicine, pediatrics, and psychiatry); residency in diagnostic laboratories and careers of physician-scientists; and for careers in epidemiology, health administration, public health, and preventive medicine. Each path would consist of a three-year preclinical portion and one-year clerkship rotations.

By departing radically from traditional medical education, this proposal leaves many unresolved questions that reduce the likelihood of its implementation. A more realistic proposal would be redesigning curricula along personalized learning pathways based on students' career plans. Personalized learning (also known as adaptive learning, individualized instruction, customized learning, or student-directed learning) is teaching tailored to an individual learner's needs, abilities, preferences, and goals, and continuously adapted to his/her evolving skills and knowledge.

A personalized learning approach can increase learner motivation and engagement (Shemshack and Spector 2020). A 2021 systematic review found that most studies focused on student "interests" and "needs." Student achievement, perception, and satisfaction were the most common outcomes, and most studies examining these outcomes found a positive relationship between them and personalized learning (Bernacki et al. 2021). I know of no attempts to introduce individualized learning into medical education.

9.3 Furthering Student Well-being

As early as, Atkinson noted that clinical tutors differ between those who view students as progressing along an obstacle course and those who view students as colleagues to be "treated in an egalitarian manner and ... groomed for their full professional status as soon as possible" (Atkinson 1973). As discussed in Chaps. 3 and 4, students' assessments of their learning environment vary across medical schools. These assessments correlate with student learning, preparation for practice, and well-being and are inversely related to burnout. Clear expectations, autonomy, and frequent feedback were cited as desirable features of the clinical learning environment, while tutors' disinterest in students, dismissal of questions, lack of autonomy, and unclear expectations led to student withdrawal and vulnerability (Barret and Scott 2019; McClintock et al. 2022).

Therefore, medical education should provide students with well-being initiatives, psychological and emotional support resources (Slavin 2019), and a constructive relationship with their clinical tutors (Benbassat 2014). It would appear to me that the longitudinal integrated clerkships (Chap. 5) are the best way to meet this challenge. They provide students with one-on-one mentoring that promotes viewing students as colleagues rather than being continuously reminded of their status in the clinical hierarchy as in some hospital-based block clerkships (Dube et al. 2019; Buery-Joyner et al. 2019).

9.4 Managing Time-Constrained Doctor-Patient Encounters[3]

Medical training emphasizes a thorough history, system review, head-to-toe examination, and a problem-oriented record. However, I am not aware of attempts to teach how to practice when time constraints preclude a comprehensive "patient work-up."

---

[3] A previous version of this sub-section was published in Benbassat J. Managing time-constrained doctor-patient encounters: A proposal for a teaching program by a former doctor and present patient. Journal of Primary Care and General Practice, 3 (1). 2020:1–3. (Open access).

9.4 Managing Time-Constrained Doctor-Patient Encounters

In the absence of teaching, medical graduates devise shortcuts that may be dysfunctional. This subsection draws attention to these shortcuts and suggests a set of priorities in data gathering in time-constrained encounters with patients (Benbassat 2020).

The main doctors' error is an attempt to save time by interrupting the patient's narrative after an average of 11 s by asking a closed question (Singh Ospina et al. 2019). Whether this behavior is timesaving is uncertain; however, it probably contributes to patient complaints that the doctor "did not listen" or "ignored my concerns." As detailed in Sect. 8.1, failure to identify a patient's concerns precludes empathy and reduces doctors' ability to respond to patient's expectations.

A second error is doctors interacting with the computer at the beginning of the encounter and performing a screen-guided system review. A system review has been shown to lead to new diagnoses in 5–10% of patients (Mitchell et al. 1992; Boland et al. 1995; Verdon and Siemens 1997). However, it may also provide irrelevant information, and novices may perform the systems review as a substitute for listening to a patient's narrative. Like interpreters, computers introduce a third party into the examination room: interpreters and computer screens compete with the patient for the doctor's attention, and the doctor should reduce the awareness of their presence. Yet, many doctors enhance the presence of interpreters by talking to them rather than to the patient. Similarly, many doctors increase the awareness of the presence of the electronic record by focusing on the screen as soon as greeting the patient and performing a screen-driven interrogation (Patel et al. 2002). Such an interrogation inhibits patients' narratives; diminishes doctors' responsiveness to patients' cues about psychosocial issues and emotional concerns; prevents eye contact and observing the patient's body language; and forces doctors to interview in a disease-centered style.

To reduce these errors, students should be advised to (a) Postpone viewing the electronic medical record until the end of the encounter; (b) Listen to the patient's narrative for 2–3 min, rather than interrupting it within seconds. The review of systems may be replaced by open questions such as, "Is there something else that has been bothering you?"; (c) If needed, perform a focused, rather than a head-to-toe physical examination; and (d) Conclude the encounter by updating the electronic record while sitting at the patient's side, thereby combining patient education with keeping his/her electronic health record (White and Danis 2013). Inviting patients to view their record not only avoids uncomfortable periods of silence; it ensures the patient's agreement on her/his story, concerns and expectations, and the patient's understanding of the doctor's assessment and advice for further examinations and treatment; it promotes patients' education, shared decision making, and patients' feeling in control of his/her care. Time constraints permit only a problem-oriented summary of the patient's subjective concerns, relevant objective findings, assessment, and plan. For example: "Mrs. T reports sore throat, cough, and runny nose of two days duration. She fears a lung infection and expects a thorough examination and possibly also a chest x-ray and antibiotic Rx. On examination fever of 36.7°C, respiratory rate 16/min, no abnormalities in the throat, lungs, maxillary, and frontal sinuses. Assessment: probable viral upper respiratory infection. Pt reassured that a chest X-ray and antibiotic Rx are not indicated and advised to take paracetamol as needed."

Individuals who were initially trained in the absence of time constraints performed more accurately in realistic conditions than those who were trained from the beginning under conditions of time constraints (Gonzalez and Brunstein 2009). In other words, training for high-time-pressure tasks is more effective if initially performed at a slow pace. Rather than begin training under realistic conditions, medical students should initially be trained at a slow pace and be exposed to time-constrained conditions only after mastering the skills.

9.5 Teaching the Social and Behavioral Sciences[4]

The undisputed evidence that the primary determinants of health inequities are social, rather than biomedical (Clouston and Link 2021) has led to including the behavioral and social sciences (BSS) into the undergraduate medical curricula. However, the early attempts in the 1970s to implement BSS courses encountered sustained student dissatisfaction: they appeared to "be bored by information with which they agree, and reject information with which they disagree" (Antonovsky 1987); they found behavioral science irrelevant to medical practice (Van-Egeren and Fabrega 1976); they were "somewhat contemptuous of the study of social medicine" and believed that "the relationships between psychosocial factors and health are either so obvious that they require little explanation, or so fanciful that they ... exist only as psychiatric or sociological delusions" (Rakoff 1984), and as recently as 2022 the implementation of BSS courses remains problematic (Dikomitis et al. 2022). BSS programs have been subject to revision, discontinued courses, high teacher turnover, and changes in course directors.

In my experience, problem-based BSS learning in small groups is not only more effective than lectures; it is the *only* way to get the message across. I subscribe to the view that the use of scenarios of realistic cases is more effective than lecture-based methods in improving knowledge retention, communication skills, problem-solving skills, and self-learning skills, and is associated with higher learner satisfaction (Trullàs et al. 2022). Rather than *lecturing to the entire class,* attempts to teach the BSS should challenge *small groups of students* to discuss possible problems they may encounter in clinical practice. By allowing students to set their own pace, they generally recognize the same goals the teacher had in mind, albeit in a slightly different order.

I suggest focusing teaching the BSS on two objectives. The first one is to change students' attitudes, unconscious adherence to stereotypes, and tendency to dismiss the complaints of patients with mental health problems, recent life events, loneliness, low socioeconomic status, substance dependence, and belonging to an ethnic minority (see Sect. 8.1.3). The second objective of teaching the BSS is patient

---

[4] A previous version of this section was published in Benbassat J, Baumal R, Borkan JM, Ber R. Overcoming barriers to teaching the behavioral and social sciences to medical students. Academic Medicine. 2003 Apr 1;78(4):372–80. With permission through the Copyright Clearance Center.

interviewing and counseling. Asking students *ex-cathedra* to be polite to patients will likely be taken for granted at best. At worst, it may be seen as insulting, and elicit resistance. However, if small groups of students are asked to list the most common patient complaints about physicians, students find that many physicians may indeed be rude to patients (Benbassat and Baumal 2001). Similarly, lecturing students to show patients respect is likely to be taken for granted or perceived as insulting. However, small groups of students react differently when asked to counsel hypothetical patients of low and high standing. Then they find that they are not immune to stereotyping (Benbassat and Baumal 2002).

9.6 Teaching Clinical Reasoning and Coping with Uncertainty

My undergraduate education in the 1950s did not include clinical reasoning. At that time, uncertainty was rarely acknowledged. Clinical reasoning was guided by pathophysiologic rationale and unsystematic personal experience, which doctors translated into intuitive decisions. The advantage of intuitive decisions is that they are quick and usually correct. In the 1950s, they satisfied clinical needs, and doctors were not aware that they needed improvement. Only in the 1970s, the high frequency of medical error (Berner and Graber 2008) and unexplained variations in clinical practice (Keating et al. 2018) indicated that intuition may go wrong. Consequently, the continuum of reasoning, critical thinking, problem-solving, and decision-making became the subject of scientific scrutiny (Elstein et al. 1978) and attempts to share it with medical students (Custers 2013; Lambe et al. 2016).

The goal of these attempts was to impart to students the reasoning strategies used by experts and a recognition of situations in which these strategies may fail (Eva 2005). However, teaching clinical reasoning is a relatively recent addition to medical education and the optimal methods for teaching it remain uncertain. As late as 2020, it was acknowledged that "…the creation of explicit, theory-informed clinical reasoning curricula… and assessment tools has proceeded slowly" (Connor et al. 2020), and only 28% of 313 medical schools from 76 countries reported that they teach clinical reasoning (Kononowicz et al. 2020).

A reasonable approach to teaching clinical reasoning would include the application of Bayes' theorem to diagnosis, risk-benefit analysis to treatment, and evidence-based medicine to the evaluation of information. I suggest that students' clinical reasoning could be enhanced by replacing the head-to-toe teaching approach to the physical examination with the hypothesis-driven patient examination, providing students with an insight into the deliberations and doubts of their preceptors, gaining an insight into the specific difficulties in learning clinical reasoning, and by providing feedback to students' summaries of the patient's problem-oriented record (problem list, relevant history, and physical examination data, differential diagnosis, hypothesis-directed diagnostic testing, and treatment plan).

9.6.1 The Hypothesis-Driven Physical Examination

Students demonstrate poor examination skills during their clerkships and on medical licensing exams (Peitzman and Cuddy 2015), and examination errors have repeatedly led to misdiagnosis and other medical errors (Russo et al. 2020). Consequently, the traditional teaching of head-to-toe physical examination has been criticized for not fully achieving its goal. Since the 1970s, there have been calls for alternative approaches to teaching it.

One of these encourages students to use the same way that a physician approaches diagnostic problems, namely by making diagnostic hypotheses and then performing a "hypothesis-driven" physical examination to test those hypotheses (Nishigori et al. 2011). Indeed, when students are confronted with clinical problems, they can form diagnostic hypotheses, and teaching interventions that promote expert reasoning are feasible at all stages of medical education. Furthermore, evidence suggests that teaching the hypothesis-driven physical examination is more effective than the head-to-toe examination (Kamel et al. 2011; Fagan et al. 2003). *The hypothesis-driven physical examination appears more effective even though it may miss an unexpected finding that could have been detected on a head-to-toe examination.*

9.6.2 Doctors' Problem-Solving Strategies

Earlier approaches to the study of clinical reasoning viewed the doctor as the source of effective or ineffective reasoning. These studies indicated that to solve problems, doctors use automatic ("pattern recognition") and controlled ("hypothetico-deductive") information processing, whereby they generate a set of diagnostic hypotheses and seek additional findings that ought to be present if they were true. Pattern recognition is the most common path of diagnostic reasoning at all levels from novices to expert clinicians (Norman et al. 2007). It resolves "easy" cases, while "complex" cases require a generation of hypotheses. Whether a case is easy, or complex depends on the doctor's experience and domain knowledge (Patel and Kaufman 2014) which develop in stages. Between novice and expert, there is an intermediate stage that is typified by considering more diagnostic hypotheses and requesting more laboratory tests than both novices (who lack the knowledge to conduct irrelevant searches) and experts (who are more parsimonious than intermediates in their differential diagnosis). Experts perform better in their domain than those outside of their domain, and this suggests a four-stage theory: novices, intermediate students, generic experts, and domain experts (Patel and Kaufman 2014). *Studies of expert-novice differences and the biases that may affect clinical reasoning will probably improve the approach to teaching the continuum of reasoning, critical thinking, problem-solving, and decision-making.*

9.6.3 Barriers to Learning Clinical Reasoning

The main difficulties students may have in learning clinical reasoning are related to the uncertain methods of its assessment, the incompatibilities between the determinism of basic science and the probabilistic reasoning required for clinical decision-making, and possibly also, the culture of the hectic hospital clinical learning environment that may impede students' development of tolerance of uncertainty.

One of the goals of the undergraduate medical curriculum is to provide its graduates with the ability to cope with the uncertainty of clinical practice. However, as discussed in Chap. 1, it is uncertain how to promote students' epistemological development and tolerance of uncertainty. Piaget et al. (2014) suggested that understanding uncertainty grows out of understanding physical causality. This is consistent with the sequence of the undergraduate medical curriculum: students understand the cause-effect relationships taught by the sciences; recognize the limitations of scientific laws in predicting the future; and lastly develop a tolerance to uncertainty and adopt concepts of stochastic causality. The biomedical sciences equip the learner with a framework of knowledge within which causal relations between phenomena may be comprehended. Thus, they provide a structure for considering ill-structured problems. Later, students will become accustomed to the reality of clinical medicine when confronted with cases that do not fit within the biomedical model.

Approaches to teaching clinical reasoning should consider student's cognitive, cultural, and environmental factors. At the *cognitive* level, medical students must come to terms first, with the shift in education from being heavily scientific-oriented to including relevant topics from the behavioral sciences, particularly in medicine, family medicine, and psychiatry (Schuwirth and van der Vleuten 2006). Second, with the transition from the cause-effect approach of the basic sciences (what happened? What caused the disease?) that requires deterministic thinking in terms of right/wrong, to prescriptive decisions in clinical practice (what will happen? what treatment may improve this patient's predicament?) that require probability estimates (Eva et al. 2007). Third, with the inconsistency between the traditional "head-to-toe" examination that students are taught and the hypothesis-driven patient examination by their clinical preceptors.

At the *cultural* level, students differ in their response to uncertainty. A 1992 review of the literature concluded that "denial of uncertainty was one of the most consistent observations made by sociologists studying medical training" (Gerrity et al. 1992) and as late as 2011, it was claimed that a discrepancy existed between the uncertainties of clinical practice and their denial in teaching settings (Luther and Crandal 2011). Finally, at the *environmental* level, it has been hypothesized that the clinical teaching environment impedes students' development of moral reasoning, empathy, and tolerance of uncertainty (Benbassat 2018).

9.6.4 Assessment of Clinical Reasoning

Another barrier to teaching and learning clinical reasoning is the difficulties in its assessment. Since there is no gold standard for clinical reasoning, several assessment methods have been proposed and evaluated by their logic, feasibility, reliability, and appeal to students (ten Cate et al. 2018). These methods fall into three broad categories: non-workplace assessments (multiple-choice questions, extended matching questions, creating decision trees that mirror illness scripts, discussing written clinical cases, script concordance test - SCT); assessments in simulated clinical environments (objective structured clinical examinations and technology-enhanced simulations); and workplace-based assessments (direct observations, global assessments, oral case presentations, written notes) (Daniel et al. 2019).

The main difficulty in implementing these methods is first, the influence of context specificity of the clinical problems: student performance on a given clinical problem does not predict that on another problem (Elstein 2009). Second, there is wide variation among assessors of clinical reasoning, and only repeated assessments can provide reliable results. Third, some assessment methods require significant investment in the application and training of faculty. Fourth, attempts to validate these methods have found varying degrees of association between them, suggesting that each measures different components of the construct of clinical reasoning (Covin et al. 2020).

Finally, recent research has indicated that reasoning is not only a cognitive endeavor but also a contextually situated and socially mediated activity, and that contextual factors (e.g., the setting of the doctor-patient encounter; patient's verbal proficiency, emotional volatility, or suggestions) can affect clinical reasoning. Evidence also suggests that this influence is not uniform; and that a doctor may or may not be aware of it (Durning et al. 2011). I know of no attempt to incorporate the interactions between the clinician and contextual factors into the assessment of clinical reasoning.

9.6.5 Summing Up

At present, it seems that teaching clinical reasoning should continue to offer programs, such as applying Bayes' theorem, risk-benefit analyses, and evidence-based medicine; the hypothesis-driven patient examination; using pattern recognition, switching back to hypothetico-deductive reasoning when faced with complexity or uncertainty; and using decision support systems that can assist in pattern recognition and differential diagnoses.

The clinical environment that promotes teaching clinical reasoning should provide medical students first, with preceptors who exhibit visibility of their deliberations, and who help students understand that doubts do not reflect incompetence but are rather the essence of clinical practice. Second, with opportunities to exercise diagnostic reasoning, observe long-term patients' outcomes, and experience a continuous relationship with their preceptor. Third, with feedback to students' summaries of the patient's problem-oriented record (problem list, relevant history, physical examination data, differential diagnosis, hypothesis-directed diagnostic testing, and treatment plan). Here again, longitudinal integrated clerkships in community settings provide students with opportunities to become familiar with a wide range of disease patterns, deliberate in a non-hectic clinical environment, and obtain a better insight into the thinking and doubts of their preceptors.

Future research may focus on the effect of helping students become aware of contextual factors that may affect clinical decision-making; one-on-one teaching and assessments in outpatient settings instead of small-group teaching and assessments in the hospital setting: and imparting attitudes to medical error. Today, most medical schools do not offer any instruction on this subject. Errors are seldom discussed, and by implication are assumed not to occur to competent physicians. The attitude to medical error will have to change to an exploration of the causes of the error aiming to make the health care system as error-proof as possible.

9.7 Dealing with Unprofessional Behavior

The American Board of Internal Medicine, the American College of Physicians–American Society of Internal Medicine, and the European Federation of Internal Medicine defined in 2002 "professionalism" as "the basis of medicine's contract with society." This definition included three principles: patient welfare, patient autonomy, and social justice but not "unprofessional" behaviors.

Recognizing the ambiguity in what is considered unprofessional, students in one of the Chicago medical schools developed a 27-item questionnaire based on their experiences of unprofessional behaviors in clinical rotations (Reddy et al. 2007). Such behaviors included inappropriate dress, violations of hospital policy (discussing patient information in public places), disregard for education (arriving late to rounds), disregard for patients and staff (making fun of patients, peers, or staff), misrepresentation (not correcting someone who mistakes you for a physician), and personal demeanor (competition with other students). Behaviors ranged from egregious (making fun of patients) to discourteous (wearing a dirty white coat) to controversial (attending pharmaceutical dinners). This questionnaire was applied in a 2007 survey that asked third-year students to report observation, participation, and perceptions of unprofessional behaviors before and 5 months after clerkships. This survey indicated that 5 months of exposure to clinical medicine changed student perceptions of unprofessional behaviors. Increased participation was seen in almost all areas and was associated with an enhanced likelihood of viewing the behaviors as acceptable. Students may feel forced to choose between the ideals of professionalism and the reality of educational survival in a hierarchical learning environment (Reddy et al. 2007).

A 2016 systematic review using the keywords *medical student, resident,* and *doctor,* AND cheating, falsification, *dishonesty, plagiarism, misrepresentation,* and *fraud,* found 51 publications. Cheating on examinations was reported between 2 and 58% of the students; listing fraudulent publications was found in 9% of the applications for residencies and plagiarism in 5%; inaccurately reporting that a medical examination was performed on a patient was found in 60% of the videotaped students; a survey of 57 psychiatry clerkship coordinators found that at most institutions (70%), one to three medical students exhibited unprofessional behavior warranting intervention on an annual basis. Concerning residents, as many as 43% falsely reported duty hours, and 45% reported directly observing other residents falsifying clinical and other records; 74% reported observing the mistreatment of patients by colleagues, and 73% reported witnessing colleagues working in an impaired condition (Fargen et al. 2016). A 2010 survey of interns at three Chicago medicine residencies found that 19% reported making fun of patients and 11% reported falsifying patient records (Arora et al. 2010).

These findings indicate a need for improving professionalism among medical students, interns, and residents. As I stated earlier, this would include debriefing learners about challenging situations they have encountered in a non-judgmental atmosphere of respect and acknowledgment that none of us is immune from unprofessional behavior. Periodic assessment of the medical school learning environment, as required by the Liaison Committee on Medical Education, can ensure that student exposure to unprofessional behavior is minimized.

9.8 Teamwork

The advances in medical knowledge and biotechnology preclude health care provision by a single person. Today health care at all levels and sites is provided by teams of care providers and the ability to work in teams is an essential requirement of medical school graduates.

The medical ethical codes include the relationship between doctors, their colleagues, and other care providers on the team. The US Code refers to the requirement of truth reporting; treating subordinates with respect, refraining from abusing, humiliating, and exploiting them; and reporting an impaired colleague with a physical or mental illness, addiction, lack of awareness of professional standards, or morally inappropriate professional behavior. The ethical codes of the USA and Canada emphasize the duty of the employing institution to help impaired physicians by providing medical treatment in case of illness or retraining in the case of a deficient skill. There are deficiencies in abiding by these three requirements, and I am embarrassed to admit that I have occasionally violated them. Surveys have shown that doctors are sometimes willing to deceive patients, insurance companies, and patients' relatives if the lie benefits the patient.

The fourth element of teamwork is the requirement to avoid abuse of authority. This requirement is also not fully implemented. As recently as 2019, student humiliation (Barret and Scott 2019) and neglect (Buery-Joyner et al. 2019) by faculty were reported to be common in clinical settings. As recently as 2022, it was asserted that "many of the fundamental components of psychological safety are lacking in the current clinical learning environments for medical students" (McClintock et al. 2022). It is impossible to ignore student distress and still teach them how to manage patient distress. It is impossible to humiliate medical students and still teach them how to respect patients.

There is also an unwillingness to comply with the fifth element of peer relations, which is the obligation to report an impaired colleague, e.g., with depression and alcohol or drug addiction. Impaired doctors tend to deny their condition. The denial may reflect their desire to "deal alone" or may stem from shame and prejudice towards mental illness and addiction. In any case, a doctor who has devoted years to his professional training will not be willing to admit, even to himself, that he is not qualified. Therefore, many of us react with hostility to any offer of help thereby creating a bond of silence. I know of two heads of department in a large hospital who were addicted to alcohol for more than a decade. This was known to the administrators, to the doctors in the hospital, and to most patients, who smelled the alcohol emanating from them during rounds. As far as I know, nothing was done about it, and they both retired on time. The recommended response to a doctor's impairment is forced leave and help in obtaining treatment.

The last requirement is to refrain from derogatory criticism of colleagues. In the 1950s and 1960s, doctors occasionally expressed in the patient's presence their contempt for the referring doctor either because of unjustified or late referral. In the USA, the term "consultant terror" was used to refer to the fear of defamatory criticism by a consultant about the treatment the patient had received so far. Today such events are less common than in the 1960s and 1970s. However, occasionally they occur as criticism in the daily press of the government's efforts to contain the Covid epidemic (Benbassat 2024).

So far, I have mentioned situations that leave no room for doubt. However, sometimes the clinical reality creates vague situations. For example, it is not always clear where is the line between respecting a colleague and criticizing him/her when appropriate. Sometimes there are clear standards for professional or ethical judgment and sometimes—not. There is no doubt that a doctor with chronic dysfunction should be treated. However, is there an obligation to investigate a one-time error in the clinical judgment of an otherwise competent colleague? Assisted suicide is an ethical offense in the eyes of many, but not in the eyes of others. I suppose that most of us would define as medical malpractice the postponement of the diagnosis of breast cancer, while adhering to a wrong diagnostic concept, for a year. But what about 2 months? Weeks? days? All these difficulties stem from the fact that retrospective evaluation of clinical decisions does not require categorical thinking in the right/wrong style, but rather probabilistic thinking in terms of more likely or less likely.

9.9 Private Care in Countries with Universal Health Insurance[5]

Most European countries provide their citizens with universal health insurance while allowing care providers to attend to private and public patients. I use the term "private care" to refer to the purchase of health services whether included in the basic package of benefits or not, whether in private or public settings, paid directly by the patient or by his/her supplementary or private insurance, or involving gifts or contributions to institutions or research projects.

A 2007 study of the interaction between public and private healthcare provision in a National Health Service (NHS), with free public care and costly private care, indicated that allowing physician dual practice "crowds out" public provision and *results in lower overall healthcare provision* (Brekke and Sørgard 2007). In Israel, the 1995 National Health Insurance law legitimized private practice by stipulating that persons can purchase extended insurance for medical services not included in the basic benefits package. By 2012, private spending represented 37% of national health expenditures in Israel (OECD 2015 Health Systems). Other countries with universal health insurance have adopted similar mixed public-private healthcare funding models (Schmid et al. 2010).

This subsection focuses on the problems emerging when the same care provider attends to private and public patients. Specifically, I question whether public hospitals that allow their doctors to attend to private patients provide an appropriate learning environment for medical students and residents. I conclude by proposing a complete separation between the public and the private healthcare systems.

9.9.1 Ethical Issues

The medical ethics code includes the principles of non-maleficence, beneficence, respect for patient autonomy, and distributive justice (Beauchamp and Childress 2001). Ethical dilemmas, i.e., situations in which doctors cannot abide by one ethical principle without violating another, have always existed. However, since the 1970s, the shifts from doctors' paternalism to respect for patient autonomy and from uncontrolled to parsimonious utilization of care resources have produced a range of previously unrecognized dilemmas.

On the one hand, private care responds to the requirement to respect patients' autonomy by deferring to their willingness to pay for care. Part of the payments for private care are channeled to the hospital, with subsequent benefits for all patients.

---

[5] A previous version of this sub-section was published in Benbassat J. Provision of Private Care by Doctors Employed in Public Health Institutions: Ethical Considerations and Implications for Clinical Training. The Israel Medical Association Journal: IMAJ. 2015 Jun 1;17(6):335–8. With permission from the editor.

On the other hand, private care violates the principle of equity. Equity requires that access to medical care and the choice of clinical interventions be guided by patients' needs only, irrespective of ability to pay or likelihood of benefit for the patient. The likelihood of benefit should certainly guide patient triage in emergencies or admission to intensive care units. However, in non-emergent clinical settings, equity prevails on other ethical principles, such as utilitarianism (priority for those most likely to benefit from health care) and respect for patient autonomy (in choosing a private health provider). Second, private care competes with public care for doctors' time and energy. Therefore, respect for patients' right to pay for rapid access to specific care providers infringes on the rights of other patients.

9.9.2 Other Issues

Health care is a public service. Just as it would be unthinkable that police officers be permitted to function as private detectives, so also provision of private care by doctors employed in public hospitals may erode patient trust in the health care system. Furthermore, care providers who attend to private and public patients communicate a message that the care they deliver to public patients is inferior.

Indeed, there are indications that private patients in the hospitals in Jerusalem receive preferential surgical care (Ofer et al. 2006) and are more satisfied than public patients (Carmel and Halevy 1999). In attempting to reduce waiting time in the public sector, physicians in private practice may even have a conflict of interest because the longer the wait in the public sector the greater the attraction to the private sector. Finally, the permission to attend to public and private patients has led to the present situation, whereby doctors enjoy the security of tenured employment in elite public institutions, the prestige of academic degrees, and the added income from private care.

9.9.3 Private Care in Public Institutions: Effect on Role Modeling

Role modeling is a powerful teaching strategy, as many medical graduates remember role models who shaped their professional attitudes. Role modeling occurs in a defined learning environment, institutional culture, and "hidden curriculum," i.e., the cultural mores that are transmitted but not openly acknowledged. Students' observations of behaviors and role modeling have been claimed to affect learning more than formal teaching "not only because [they are] reinforced more frequently, but because [they] relate to doing rather than saying" (Treadway and Chatterjee 2011).

What messages does a learning environment project to medical trainees who observe their role models providing care to private and public patients? There is undisputed evidence that healthcare providers unintentionally and unconsciously discriminate among patients. For example, white patients have better access than Afro-American patients to specialized services (Coulehan and Williams 2001). However, a learning environment that approves role models who attend to private and public patients may also provide legitimacy to deliberate and conscious patient discrimination (Benbassat 2015).

9.9.4 "Black" Medicine

The possibility of extended coverage within public institutions of health care may blur the boundaries between legal and illegal fees for service, and private care in public hospitals may degenerate into black medicine (Cohen 2012). "Black medicine" refers to informal payments for care that include illegal activities such as bribing a doctor and marginal actions such as giving a gift to a doctor or contributing to his/her department to obtain better treatment. It has been estimated that informal payments comprise 1.5–4.5% of total healthcare expenditures in Hungary, 30% in Poland, 56% in the Russian Federation, 84% in Azerbaijan (Filc and Cohen 2014), and 14% in Israel (Cohen 2012).

9.9.5 Suggestions for Improvement

A possible way to maintain the advantages of private care and still avoid its negative consequences would be to separate the public and private healthcare sectors. Just as a police officer may open a private detective office only after resigning from the police force, so also physicians may attend to private patients, or hold other medical jobs only after resigning from public hospitals. This suggestion is consistent with the recommendations of the 2007 study I referred to earlier (Brekke and Sørgard 2007).

9.10 Evaluation and Counseling of Medical School Graduates

Summative evaluations of medical school graduates typically follow the three steps of the United States Medical Licensing Examination (USMLE). Step 1 is a multiple-choice exam that tests how well the examinee applies basic and scientific concepts to clinical scenarios. Step 2 is a multiple-choice exam. It determines whether the examinee has the medical knowledge required to provide patient care under supervision. Step 2 also includes a practical examination that tests the examinee's ability to gather information from standardized patients, perform a physical examination, communicate the findings to the patient, and write a patient report. Step 3 is a multiple-choice exam that tests the ability to apply medical knowledge, focusing on patient management in the outpatient setting. It attempts to test students' ability to synthesize, analyze, and apply data, rather than their ability to recall.

I suggest supplementing these assessments in the final year of medical school with Multiple Mini Interviews (MMIs) (Pau et al. 2013), Situational Judgement Tests (SJTs) (De Leng et al. 2017), and personality tests. This would certainly be much more cost-effective than conducting them on all medical school applicants. The results of these tests would serve as a starting point for individualized feedback on students' performance during the clerkship rotations and for counseling on students' potential strengths and weaknesses in specific subject areas. The providers of feedback and counseling would emphasize the limitations of MMIs, SJTs, SCs, and personality tests and address the "dark sides" of conscientiousness, empathy, and emotional intelligence. The main purpose of this final interaction between students and teachers would be to discuss possible career alternatives in an atmosphere where students are not judged but trusted and supported in their deliberations.

References

Adam J, Bore M, Childs R, Dunn J, Mckendree J, Munro D, et al. Predictors of professional behavior and academic outcomes in a UK medical school: a longitudinal cohort study. Med Teach. 2015;37:868–80.

Admissions to Higher Education Steering Group. Fair admissions to higher education: recommendations for good practice. Nottingham: Dept for Education and Skills Publications; 2007. http://www.admissions-review.org.uk.

Albanese MA, Snow MH, Skochelak SE, Huggett KN, Farrell PM. Assessing personal qualities in medical school admissions. Acad Med. 2003;78:313–21.

Antonovsky A. The fluctuating fortunes of the behavioral sciences. Isr J Med Sci. 1987;23:1022–6.

Arora VM, Wayne DB, Anderson RA, Didwania A, Farnan JM, Reddy ST, Humphrey HJ. Changes in perception of and participation in unprofessional behaviors during internship. Acad Med. 2010;85(10):S76–80.

Atkinson P. Worlds apart. Learning environments in medicine and surgery. Br J Med Educ. 1973;7:218–24.

Barret J, Scott KM. Acknowledging medical students' reports of intimidation and humiliation by their teachers in hospitals. J Pediatr Child Health. 2019;55:125–251.

Beauchamp T, Childress J. Principles of biomedical ethics. 5th ed. Oxford: Oxford University Press; 2001.

Benbassat J. Role modeling in medical education: the importance of a reflective imitation. Acad Med. 2014;89(4):550–4.

Benbassat J. Provision of private care by doctors employed in public health institutions: ethical considerations and implications for clinical training. IMAJ. 2015;17(6):335–8.

Benbassat J. Hypothesis: the hospital learning environment impedes students' acquisition of reflectivity and medical professionalism. Adv Health Sci Educ. 2018;24:185–94.

Benbassat J. Managing time-constrained doctor-patient encounters: a proposal for a teaching program by a former doctor and present patient. J Prim Care Gen Pract. 2020;3(1):1–3.

Benbassat J. Trust in public health policy in the time of the COVID-19 epidemic in Israel. Isr J Health Policy Res. 2024;13(1):24.

Benbassat J, Baumal R. Teaching doctor-patient interviewing skills using an integrated learner and teacher-centered approach. Am J Med Sci. 2001;322:349–57.

Benbassat J, Baumal R. A stepwise role-playing approach for teaching patient counseling skills to medical students. Patient Educ Couns. 2002;46:147–52.

Benbassat J, Baumal R. What Is Empathy, and How Can It Be Promoted during Clinical Clerkships? Acad Med. 2004;79:832–839.

Benbassat J, Baumal R. Expected benefits of streamlining undergraduate medical education by an early commitment to specific medical specialties. Adv Health Sci Educ. 2012;17:145–55.

Benor DE, Notzer N, Sheehan TJ, Norman GR. Moral reasoning as a criterion for admission to medical school. Med Educ. 1984;18(6):423–8.

Bernacki ML, Greene MJ, Lobczowski NG. A systematic review of research on personalized learning: personalized by whom, to what, how, and for what purpose (s)? Educ Psychol Rev. 2021;33:1675–715.

Berner ES, Graber ML. Overconfidence as a cause of diagnostic error in medicine. Am J Med. 2008;121(5 Suppl):S2–23.

Boland BJ, Wollan PC, Silverstein MD. Review of systems, physical examination, and routine tests for case-finding in ambulatory patients. Am J Med Sci. 1995;309(4):194–200.

Bore M, Munro D, Kerridge I, Powis D. Selection of medical students according to their moral orientation. Med Educ. 2005;39:266–75.

Brekke KR, Sørgard L. Public versus private health care in a national health service. Health Econ. 2007;16(6):579–601.

Brotherton SE, Simon FA, Etzel SI. US graduate medical education, 2000–2001. JAMA. 2001;286:1056–60.

Buery-Joyner SD, Ryan MS, Santen SA, Borda A, Webb T, Cheifetz C. Beyond mistreatment: learner neglect in the clinical teaching environment. Med Teach. 2019;41:949–55.

Carmel S, Halevy J. Patient satisfaction and hospital services evaluation: comparison of public and private patients. Harefuah. 1999;137:363–70. (Hebrew)

Carrothers RM, Gregory SW, Gallagher TJ. Measuring emotional intelligence of medical school applicants. Acad Med. 2000;75:456–63.

Clouston SAP, Link BG. A retrospective on fundamental cause theory: state of the literature, and goals for the future. Annu Rev Sociol. 2021;47:131–56.

Cohen N. Informal payments for healthcare—the phenomenon and its context. Health Econ Policy Law. 2012;7:285–308.

Collins JP, White GR, Petrie KJ, Willoughby EW. A structured panel interview and group exercise in the selection of medical students. Med Educ. 1995;29:332–6.

Connor DM, Durning SJ, Rencic JJ. Clinical reasoning as a core competency. Acad Med. 2020;95:1166–71.

Cook CJ, Cook CE, Hilton TN. Does emotional intelligence influence success during medical school admissions and program matriculation? A systematic review. J Educ Eval Health Prof. 2016;13:40.

Coulehan J, Williams PC. Vanquishing virtue: the impact of medical education. Acad Med. 2001;76:598–605.

Covin Y, Longo P, Wick N, Gavinski K, Wagner J. Empirical comparison of three assessment instruments of clinical reasoning capability in 230 medical students. BMC Med Educ. 2020;20:264.

Custers EJFM. Medical education and cognitive continuum theory: an alternative perspective on medical problem solving and clinical reasoning. Acad Med. 2013;88:1074–80.

Daniel M, Rencic J, Durning SJ, Holmboe E, Santen SA, Lang V, Ratcliffe T, Gordon D, Heist B, Lubarsky S, Estrada CA. Clinical reasoning assessment methods: a scoping review and practical guidance. Acad Med. 2019;94:902–12.

De Leng WE, Stegers-Jager KM, Husbands A, Dowell JS, Born M, Themmen APN. Scoring method of a situational judgment test: influence on internal consistency reliability, adverse impact and correlation with personality? Adv Health Sci Educ. 2017;22:243–65.

Dikomitis L, Wenning B, Ghobrial A, Adams KM. Embedding behavioral and social sciences across the medical curriculum:(auto) ethnographic insights from medical schools in the United Kingdom. Societies. 2022;12(4):101.

Donnon T, Paolucci EO, Violato C. The predictive validity of the MCAT for medical school performance and medical board licensing examinations: a meta-analysis of the published research. Acad Med. 2007;82(1):100–6.

Dube T, Schinke R, Strasser R. It takes a community to train a future physician: social support experienced by medical students during a community-engaged longitudinal integrated clerkship. Can Med Educ J. 2019;10:e5–e16.

Durning S, Artino AR, Pangaro L, van der Vleuten CPM, Schuwirth L. Context and clinical reasoning: understanding the perspective of the expert's voice. Med Educ. 2011;45:927–38.

Elstein AS. Thinking about diagnostic thinking: a 30-year perspective. Adv Health Sci Educ. 2009;14:7–18.

Elstein AS, Shulman LS, Sprafka SA. Medical problem solving: an analysis of clinical reasoning. Cambridge, MA: Harvard University Press; 1978.

Eva KW. What every teacher needs to know about clinical reasoning. Med Educ. 2005;39:98–106.

Eva KW, Rosenfeld J, Reiter HI, Norman GR. An admissions OSCE: the multiple mini-interview. Med Educ. 2004;38:314–26.

Eva KW, Hatala RM, VR LB, Brooks LR. Teaching from the clinical reasoning literature: combined reasoning strategies help novice diagnosticians overcome misleading information. Med Educ. 2007;41:1152–8.

Eveland AP, Wilhelm SR, Wong S, Prado LG, Barsky SH. A preliminary study of the probitive value of personality assessment in medical school admissions within the United States. BMC Med Educ. 2022;22(1):890.

Fagan MJ, Griffith RA, Obbard L, O'Connor CJ. Improving the physical diagnosis skills of third-year medical students. A controlled trial of a literature-based curriculum. J Gen Intern Med. 2003;18:652–5.

Fargen KM, Drolet BC, Philibert I. Unprofessional behaviors among tomorrow's physicians: review of the literature with a focus on risk factors, temporal trends, and future directions. Acad Med. 2016;91(6):858–64.

Feletti GI, Sanson-Fisher RW, Vidler M. Admissions Committee of the Faculty of medicine, University of Newcastle, New South Wales. Evaluating a new approach to selecting medical students. Med Educ. 1985;19(4):276–84.

Ferguson E, Lievens F. Future directions in personality, occupational and medical selection: myths, misunderstandings, measurement, and suggestions. Adv Health Sci Educ. 2017;22:387–99.

Ferguson E, James D, Madeley L. Factors associated with success in medical school: systematic review of the literature. Br Med J. 2002;324:952–7.

Ferguson E, James D, O'Hehir F, Sanders A, McManus IC. Pilot study of the roles of personality, references, and personal statements in relation to performance over the five years of a medical degree. Br Med J. 2003;326:429–32.

Filc D, Cohen N. Blurring the boundaries between public and private healthcare services as an alternative explanation for the emergence of black medicine: the Israeli case. Health Econ Policy Law. 2014;9:1–18.

Functions and Structure of a Medical School. Standards for accreditation of medical education programs leading to the M.D. Degree. 2016. https://med.virginia.edu/ume-curriculum/wp-content/uploads/sites/216/2016/07/2017-18_Functions-and-Structure_2016-03-24.pdf. Accessed July 2019.

Gafni N, Moshinsky A, Eisenberg O, Zeigler D, Ziv A. Reliability estimates: behavioral stations and questionnaires in medical school admissions. Med Educ. 2012;46:277–88.

Gerrity MS, Earp JAL, DeVellis RF, Light DW. Uncertainty and professional work: perception of physicians in clinical practice. Am J Sociol. 1992;97:1022–51.

Gonzalez C, Brunstein AP. Training for emergencies. J Trauma. 2009;67(2):S100–5.

Hadad A, Gafni N, Moshinsky A, Turvall E, Ziv A, Israeli A. The multiple mini-interviews as a predictor of peer evaluations during clinical training in medical school. Med Teach. 2016;38:1172–9.

Haight SJ, Chibnall JT, Schindler DL, Slavin SJ. Associations of medical student personality and health/wellness characteristics with their medical school performance across the curriculum. Acad Med. 2012;87:476–85.

Hamby T, Taylor W, Snowden AK, Peterson RA. A meta-analysis of the reliability of free and for-pay big five scales. J Psychol. 2016;150:422–30.

Hecker K, Norman G. Have admissions committees considered all the evidence? Adv Health Sci Educ. 2017;22:573–6.

Hojat M, Robeson M, Damjanov I, Veloski JJ, Glaser K, Gonnella JS. Students' psychosocial characteristics as predictors of academic performance in medical school. Acad Med. 1993;68(8):635–7.

Hojat M, Erdmann JB, Gonnella JS. Personality assessments and outcomes in medical education and the practice of medicine: AMEE guide no. 79. Med Teach. 2013;35:e1267–301.

Hsueh W, Wilkinson T, Bills J. What evidence-based undergraduate interventions promote rural health? N Z Med J. 2004;117(1204):U1117.

Hull AL, Glover PB, Acheson LS, Carter JR, Dick TE, Kirby AC, Lam M, Stevens DP. Medical school applicants' essays as predictors of primary care career choice. Acad Med. 1996;71(1):S37–9.

Jerant A, Henderson MC, Griffin E, Rainwater JA, Hall TR, Kelly CJ, Peterson EM, Wofsy D, Franks P. Reliability of multiple mini-interviews and traditional interviews within and between institutions: a study of five California medical schools. BMC Med Educ. 2017;17:1–6.

Julian ER. Validity of the medical college admission test for predicting medical school performance. Acad Med. 2005;80(10):910–7.

Kamel H, Dhaliwal G, Navi BB, Pease AR, Shah M, Dhand A, Johnston SC, Josephson SA. A randomized trial of hypothesis-driven vs screening neurologic examination. Neurology. 2011;77:1395–400.

Keating NL, Huskamp HA, Kouri E, Schrag D, Hornbrook MC, Haggstrom DA, Landrum MB. Factors contributing to geographic variation in end-of-life expenditures for cancer patients. Health Aff. 2018;37:1136–43.

Koenig TW, Parrish SK, Terregino CA, Williams JP, Dunleavy D, Volsch JM. Core personal competencies important to entering students' success in medical school: what are they and how could they be assessed early in the admission process? Acad Med. 2013;88:603–13.

Kononowicz AA, Hege I, Edelbring S, Sobocan M, Huwendiek S, Durning SJ. The need for longitudinal clinical reasoning teaching and assessment: results of an international survey. Med Teach. 2020;42:457–62.

Kulatunga Moruzi C, Norman GR. Validity of admissions measures in predicting performance outcomes: the contribution of cognitive and non-cognitive dimensions. Teach Learn Med. 2002;14(1):34–42.

Lakhan SE. Diversification of US medical schools via affirmative action implementation. BMC Med Educ. 2003;3:1–6.

Lambe KA, O'Reilly G, Kelly BD, Curristan S. Dual-process cognitive interventions to enhance diagnostic reasoning: a systematic review. BMJ Qual Saf. 2016;25:808–20.

Lin JC, Shin C, Greenberg PB. The impact of the medical school admissions interview: a systematic review. Can Med Educ J. 2024;15(1):68–74.

Lupu D. Estimate of current hospice and palliative medicine physician workforce shortage. J Pain Symptom Manag. 2010;40:899.

Luther VP, Crandal SJ. Commentary: ambiguity and uncertainty: neglected elements of medical education curricula? Acad Med. 2011;86:799–800.

Marrin ML, McIntosh KA, Keane D, Schmuck ML. Use of paired comparison technique to determine the most valued quality of the McMaster medical Peogram admission process. Adv Health Sci Educ. 2004;9:129–35.

McClintock AH, Fainstad TL, Jauregui J. Clinician teacher as leader: creating psychological safety in the clinical learning environment for medical students. Acad Med. 2022;97(11S):S46–53.

McLarnon MJ, Rothstein MG, Goffin RD, Rieder MJ, Poole A, Krajewski HT, Powell DM, Jelley RB, Mestdagh T. How important is personality in the selection of medical school students? Personal Individ Differ. 2017;104:442–7.

McManus IC, Smithers E, Partridge P, Keeling A, Fleming PR. A levels and intelligence as predictors of medical careers in UK doctors: 20 year prospective study. BMJ. 2003;327(7407):139–42.

McManus IC, Livingston G, Katona C. The attractions of medicine: the generic motivations of medical school applicants in relation to demography, personality, and achievement. BMC Med Educ. 2006;6:1–5.

Mitchell TL, Tornelli JL, Fisher TD, Blackwell TA, Moorman JR. Yield of the screening review of systems: a study on a general medical service. J Gen Intern Med. 1992;7:393–7.

Monroe A, Quinn E, Samuelson W, Dunleavy D, Dowd KW. An overview of the medical school admission process and use of applicant data in decision making: what has changed since the 1980s? Acad Med. 2013;88:672–81.

Niessen ASM, Meijer RR. Selection of medical students on the basis of nonacademic skills: is it worth the trouble? Clin Med. 2016;16:339–42.

Nishigori H, Masuda K, Kikukawa M, Kawashima A, Yudkowsky R, Bordage G, Otaki J. A model teaching session for the hypothesis-driven physical examination. Med Teach. 2011;33:410–7.

Norman G. The morality of medical school admissions. Adv Health Sci Educ. 2004;9:79–82.

Norman GR, Young M, Brooks L. Non-analytical models of clinical reasoning: the role of experience. Med Educ. 2007;41:1140–5.

Nowacek G, Sachs L. Demographic variables in medical school admission. Acad Med. 1990;65(3):140–4.

O'Neill LD, Korsholm L, Wallstedt B, Eika B, Hartvigsen J. Generalizability of a composite student selection program. Med Educ. 2009;43:58–65.

OECD. Health Systems at a glance. http://www.oecd.org/els/health-systems/Health-at-a-Glance-2013.pdf. 2015. Accessed Jan 2015.

Ofer G, Rosen B, Greenstein M, Benbassat J, Halevy J, Shapira S. Public and private patients in Jerusalem hospitals: who operates on whom? IMAJ. 2006;8:270–6.

Oswald FL, Schmitt N, Kim BH, Ramsay LJ, Gillespie MA. Developing a biodata measure and situational judgment inventory as predictors of college student performance. J Appl Psychol. 2004;89(2):187.

Parry J, Mathers J, Stevens A, Parsons A, Lilford R, Spurgeon P, Thomas H. Admissions processes for five year medical courses at English schools. BMJ. 2006;332(7548):1005–9.

Patel VL, Kaufman DR. Cognitive science and biomedical informatics. In: Biomedical informatics. London: Springer; 2014. p. 156. Accessed Feb 2022. 133-185.pdf (lsmuni.lt).

Patel VL, Arocha JF, Kushniruk AW. Patients' and physicians' understanding of health and biomedical concepts: relationship to the design of EMR systems. J Biomed Inform. 2002;35(1):8–16.

Patterson F, Zibarras LD. Selecting for creativity and innovation potential: implications for practice in healthcare education. Adv Health Sci Educ. 2017;22:417–28.

Patterson F, Knight A, Dowell J, Nicholson S, Cousans F, Cleland J. How effective are selection methods in medical education? A systematic review. Med Educ. 2016a;50:36–60.

Patterson F, Zibarras L, Ashworth V. Situational judgement tests in medical education and training: research, theory, and practice: AMEE guide no. 100. Med Teacher. 2016b;38:3–17.

Patterson F, Cousans F, Edwards H, Rosselli A, Nicholson S, Wright B. The predictive validity of a text-based situational judgment test in undergraduate medical and dental school admissions. Acad Med. 2017;92:1250–3.

Patterson F, Cleland J, Cousans F. Selection methods in healthcare professions: where are we now and where next? Adv Health Sci Educ. 2017b;22:229–42.

Pau A, Jeevaratnam K, Chen YS, Fall AA, Khoo C, Nadarajah VD. The multiple mini-interview (MMI) for student selection in health professions training—a systematic review. Med Teach. 2013;35:1027–41.

Peitzman SJ, Cuddy MM. Performance in physical examination on the USMLE step 2 clinical skills examination. Acad Med. 2015;90:209–13.

Perkins DN, Salomon G. Are cognitive skills context-bound? Educ Res. 1989;18:16–25.

Piaget J, Inhelder B, Fraise P, Piaget J. Intellectual operations and their development. In: Experimental psychology its scope and method: VII intelligence. Boca Raton: Taylor & Francis Group; 2014. p. 144–205. Accessed Nov 2023. Experimental Psychology Its Scope and Method: Volume VII (Psychology ...—Pierre Oléron, Jean Piaget, Bärbel Inhelder. Pierre Gréco-Google Books.

Rabinowitz HK. Recruitment, retention, and follow-up of graduates of a program to increase the number of family physicians in rural and underserved areas. N Engl J Med. 1993;328(13):934–9.

Rakoff V. The behavioral sciences and undergraduate education in psychiatry. Can J Psychiatr. 1984;29:642–7.

Reddy ST, Farnan JM, Yoon JD, Leo T, Upadhyay GA, Humphrey HJ, Arora VM. Third-year medical students' participation in and perceptions of unprofessional behaviors. Acad Med. 2007;82(10):S35–9.

Rotthoff T, Ostapczuk MS, Kroncke KD, Zimmerhofer A, Decking U, Schneider M, et al. Criterion validity of a competency-based assessment center in medical education—a 4-year follow-up study. Med Ed. 2014;19:252–4.

Russo S, Berg K, Davis J, Davis R, Riesenberg LA, Morgan C, Chambers L, Berg D. Incoming interns recognize inadequate physical examination as a cause of patient harm. J Med Educat Curri Develop. 2020;7:1–7.

Schmid A, Cacace M, Götze R, Rothgang H. Explaining health care system change: problem pressure and the emergence of "hybrid" health care systems. J Health Polit Policy Law. 2010;35:455–86.

Schuwirth LW, van der Vleuten CP. Challenges for educationalists. BMJ. 2006;333:544–6.

Shemshack A, Spector JM. A systematic literature review of personalized learning terms. Smart Learn Environ. 2020;7:1–20.

Singh Ospina N, Phillips KA, Rodriguez-Gutierrez R, Castaneda-Guarderas A, Gionfriddo MR, Branda ME, Montori VM. Eliciting the patient's agenda-secondary analysis of recorded clinical encounters. J Gen Intern Med. 2019 Jan;34:36–40.

Slavin S. Reflections on a decade leading a medical student Well-being initiative. Acad Med. 2019;94:771–4.

ten Cate O, Smal K. Educational assessment center techniques for entrance selection in medical school. Acad Med. 2002;77(7):737.

ten Cate, O. Medical education in the Netherlands. Medical Teacher. 2007;29(8):752–757.

ten Cate O, Custers EJFM, Durning SJ. Principles and practice of case-based clinical reasoning education. A method for preclinical students. Cham: Springer; 2018. Accessed in Oct 2021.

Tone EB, Tully EC. Empathy as a "risky strength": a multilevel examination of empathy and risk for internalizing disorders. Dev Psychopathol. 2014;26:1547–65.

Treadway K, Chatterjee N. Into the water—the clinical clerkships. N Engl J Med. 2011;364:1190–3.

Trullàs JC, Blay C, Sarri E, Pujol R. Effectiveness of problem-based learning methodology in undergraduate medical education: a scoping review. BMC Med Educ. 2022;22:104.

Turnbull D, Buckley P, Robinson JS, Mather G, Leahy C, Marley J. Increasing the evidence base for selection for undergraduate medicine: four case studies investigating process and interim outcomes. Med Educ. 2003;37(12):1115–20.

Van Niekerk JP. In favour of shorter medical training. SAMJ South Afr Med J. 2009;99(2):69–70.

Van-Egeren L, Fabrega H. Behavioral science and medical education: a bio-behavioral perspective. Soc Sci Med. 1976;10:535–9.

Verdon ME, Siemens K. Yield of review of systems in a self-administered questionnaire. J Am Board Fam Pract. 1997;10(1):20–7.

White A, Danis M. Enhancing patient-centered communication and collaboration by using the electronic health record in the examination room. J Am Med Ass. 2013;309(22):2327–8.

Wouters A, Croiset G, Schripsema NR, Cohen-Schotanus J, Spaai GWG, Hulsman RL, et al. A multi-site study on medical school selection, performance, motivation and engagement. Adv Health Sci Educ. 2017;22:447–62.

Zeldow PB, Preston RC, Daugherty SR. The decision to enter a medical specialty: timing and stability. Med Educ. 1992;26(4):327–32.

Index

A
Academic Freedom, 1, 4, 8, 15
Accreditation standards, 26, 37–39, 42, 43
Assessment of research productivity, 55
Attitudes, 13

B
Behavioral and social sciences (BSS), 102, 103

C
Clinician-scientists, 60, 61
Complementary alternative medicine (CAM), 69–72
Conditioning, 3
Curricular changes, 93–107
Curriculum, 25
Curriculum design
   context, 19, 20
   input, 20
   models, 16
   process, 16–19, 21
   teaching program, 13–16
Curriculum evaluation
   attitudes, 31, 32
   faculty value, 32
   instruments, 33, 34
   medical students, 32
   teaching, 25, 26
   values, 31
Curriculum mapping, 30
Curriculum models, 19

D
Diagnostic reasoning, 59

E
Early clinical program (ECP), 49
Education, 2
   support, 37
Elective model, 51
Emotional intelligence, 6
Empathy, 7
End-product evaluation, 27, 28
Epistemological Growth, 1
Evaluation, 16
Evidence-based medicine (EBM), 47, 66

F
Faculty values, 32

H
Health care, 111
Hidden curriculum, 29
Higher education, 3–5

I
Ideas, concerns and expectations (ICE), 76
Implicit curriculum, 29, 33
Important standards, 42
Indoctrination, 3
Intolerance of uncertainty, 6

K
Knowledge, 2–5, 7, 9, 13

L
Learning, 14, 15, 17, 18, 21
  atmosphere, 29
  for mastery, 79
  objectives, 8, 15
Least important standards, 43
Levels of evidence, 66
Longitudinal clerkships, 50
Longitudinal integrated clerkships (LICs), 49, 50

M
Medical education units (MEUs), 37–39, 43
Medical errors, 81–84
Moral reasoning, 6
Multiple Mini Interviews (MMIs), 113

O
Objectivism, 65

P
Patient concerns, 76
Patient expectations, 76, 86
Possibly important standards, 42
Problem-based learning (PBL), 28, 48
Problem-based model, 48
Product, 22
Professional distress, 85, 86
Professionalism, 107
p-Value Fallacy, 66

R
Randomized controlled trials (RCTs), 66
Relativism, 65
Research productivity, 57
Role models, 81

S
Science education, 58, 59
Scientific research, 59
Second opinion, 76, 77
Selection centers (SCs), 93
  of applicants, 92
Self-learning, 48
Self-study, 13, 14, 18
Skills, 13
Social influences
  health care, 67, 68
  research, 67
Student assessment, 38
Student counseling, 98, 103, 113
Student ratings, 56, 57
  of instruction, 29
Student well-being, 100

T
Teaching, 55–57, 61
  programs, 21
Team work, 108, 109

U
Underprivileged patients, 78
Universities, 4, 5, 8
Unprofessional behavior, 107, 108

Printed by Printforce, the Netherlands